D1555527

WILDERNESS LIVING

WILDERNESS LIVING

A complete handbook and guide
to pioneering in North America

by
Berndt Berglund

Illustrated by E. B. Sanders
with technical drawings
by the author

CHARLES SCRIBNER'S SONS

NEW YORK

Library of Congress Catalog Card Number 76-12888
ISBN 0-684-14747-5
Printed in the United States of America
1 3 5 7 9 11 13 15 17 19 I/C 20 18 16 14 12 10 8 6 4 2

Dedicated affectionately to my wife Clare Elaine and my daughter Santon Kim who have shared the joys and hardships with me during the process of becoming a modern settler.

Contents

Acknowledgments

Many people, experts in their fields, have made the writing of this book not only possible but by far my most gratifying experience. Their interest and generous assistance range the whole wide field of conservation and the management of our precious environment. A special thanks to governmental services and their experts in the uses and the tilling of our land. To my wife, Clare Elaine, and my secretary, Betty Thain of Campbellford, for the countless hours of critical editorial assistance and typing. To E.B. (Bev) Sanders whose line drawings have enhanced this book and to Lloyd (Bus) MacIlquham for invaluable help in the different building projects on the homestead.

Thank you all,
Berndt Berglund

EBSanders

CHAPTER 1

A Dream

Is it the fear of a depression or a recession that drives people out of the urban centers, or are people tired of being pushed around by the establishment? Judging from the mail I receive every day, I do not think it is either. I think it is a genuine desire to own a piece of land, however small, that is propelling the young and even the not-so-young to search for security and protection for their loved ones in the form of their own shelter, unpolluted water, food, and fuel.

Who can disregard the romance of log-cabin living or the slow and easy way of life on the farm or homestead? Many city-weary people want to get away from punching a timecard at office or factory but, if they did, they would soon realize that farm chores are far more demanding than any city employer. Nature and the weather will not wait until you are ready to seed or plant. The hay has to be brought in even if it is a Sunday, because tomorrow it may rain.

My wife and I for many years had been planning to make the move from the large urban center where we lived, but the dreaming and talking went on for years. Our dreams took a more concrete form one hot July day when I was sitting behind the desk in my air-conditioned office, watching the groundkeeper cutting the grass in front of my window.

Suddenly I heard a crash and the sound of falling glass — the lawnmower had picked up a stone and thrown it clear through my window. The heavenly smell of freshly cut grass came through the broken window, and my thoughts went back to the farm where I grew up. I could see myself riding the haymower down one of our fields in acres and acres of fragrant-smelling clover. The aroma of that long-ago newmown hay and the freshly cut grass outside my office window produced in me a burning desire to leave my stacks of paperwork far behind.

That same night, the subject of moving to a farm was brought up again. To my surprise, my wife and daughter were all for it. But soon I had second thoughts — although I had traveled and camped in the wilds for years, it had been many years since I had done actual farming. We would have to make many adjustments in our life style. First, we would have to get used to missing my salary that came in regardless of frost or drought. After a snowstorm could we stand the loneliness of being snowed in, cut off from all urban services; would we miss the neatly packaged meat and greens at the supermarket? Could my family stand the pet cow or hen being killed and butchered, and then be able to eat it afterwards? Would my wife hate having to go out on a cold morning to rake the coals from the outside bake oven in order to bake bread? How would we get along crowded into a small shack for the first year while building our permanent home? No radio, no television, only books, read by the light of a kerosene lamp. These are the cold realities of homesteading.

But now the enthusiasm of my family started to affect even me, although my wife's experience with farming and the country was confined to the odd vacation at her grandfather's farm, a well-organized lush fruit farm where, as the saying goes, you cut a dry branch, put it in the ground, and next thing you know you have a tree growing. I wanted to temper her enthusiasm but nothing worked. "How lovely to be miles away from a neighbor and from roads where cars are speeding up and down all the time," my wife would say. "Think how lovely it will be to track the same distance on your snowshoes to borrow a gallon of fuel oil for the lamps because you forgot to get it on your last shopping trip to the store," I would reply.

"O well," the answer would be, "we can always curl up in front of the fire for a night or so. Your eyes need a rest anyway."

"What is the matter with you? You were born and raised on a farm," was another tack, "You should know all about it."

Maybe that was the trouble — I did know, from experience, the meaning of hard, manual work from dawn until dusk — and then by lantern light. Not that it scared me, but could my family take it?

My boyhood duties included not only the usual farm chores — those connected with cows, horses, sheep, pigs, poultry, and bees, but also canning and pickling, soap and candle-making, meat-curing and wine-making. In fact, my early experiences with farm life were only slightly removed from pioneer conditions, as my grandfather believed that the farm should support the family completely. Only salt, spices, coffee, and tea were purchased from a store.

At an early age I was taught how to make tools and repair furniture; how to construct new buildings as well as repair existing ones.

12

Nails and hardware were made in the blacksmith shop; boots and leather harness were either made or repaired in our spare time during the long winter months. Wool and linen were carded and spun into thread, then woven into cloth. It was hard work but, I asked myself, had I suffered from my early years on the farm? My answer had to be a resounding no, and I was reminded of the great scientist Thomas Huxley's description of a liberal education — "That man has a liberal education who has been so trained in youth that his body is the ready servant of his will and does with ease and pleasure all the work that, as a mechanism, it is capable of; whose intellect is a clear, cold, logic engine, with all its parts of equal strength and in smooth working order, ready, like a steam engine, to turn to any kind of work, and spin the gossamer as well as forge the anchors of the mind; whose mind is stored with the great and fundamental truths of nature and of the laws of her operations; one who, no stunted ascetic, is full of life and fire, but whose passions are trained to come to heel by a vigorous will, the servant of a tender conscience; who has learned to love all beauty, whether of nature or of art, to hate all vileness and to respect others as himself."

Could I, with a clear conscience, meet my Creator if I had denied my daughter these privileges? But where can a child acquire and develop such qualities as well as on a farm; a farm well managed by loving parents able to explain and teach the laws of nature as well as the laws of the land; living in harmony with nature, their land, and their neighbors?

We then took a good look at ourselves and our more-or-less selfish and purposeless city existence. We realized that our life expectancy was shortened by tainted air, little sunshine, and by lack of exercise. We decided to leave. The decision was not an easy one but, once made, the ensuing planning and dreaming were in themselves so exhilarating it made our decision seem right.

13

CHAPTER 2

A Dream Come True

After countless weekends spent searching when my wife had packed the picnic basket and we had taken off to see yet another new discovery, we found we had not done our homework properly. Back to square one. We asked ourselves — What are we looking for? What requirements do we have for the proposed land? What are we going to do on the farm? Anybody can buy a farm but this is not all there is to it. The land has to conform to the requirements of a previously formulated plan. First, the land must be suitable for the crop or animal to be raised — berries, eggs, vegetables, chickens, ducks, or whatever. To simply buy land because one likes the look of it is no good. Next, what are you looking for — solitude, or a place close to a farming community? To help the inexperienced land buyer, here are a number of questions to ask yourself before you even start looking.

1. What do you want — solitude, or some contact with an already established community?
2. Decide on your children's educational needs. How far away can you be from the nearest school?
3. Are there good schools in the area; how do the children get there? Is there a school bus?
4. How far do you have to go to get to a doctor or a hospital?
5. Where can you do the necessary shopping?
6. In what condition are the area's roads? In winter? In the spring?
7. What about taxes? How much can you afford to pay?
8. Is there a potential market nearby for your produce? Whether you like it or not, you will have to have *some* cash.

Two more important points: Make sure you have enough working capital. Success or failure will depend on it. Also, heed the advice of the people in the immediate area where you eventually settle. What they have to say is more valuable than information in a thousand how-to books.

The next step is to decide what kind of land you need and what the land must do for you.

The basic plan for our land was based on our desire for self-sufficiency. We wanted to cultivate it, as well as utilizing the wild plants already growing there. We wanted to buy as little food as possible. We also intended to heat with our own firewood. According to our master plan, it would require more than 100 but less than 200 acres to accomplish all this. Ideally half the land would have to be fairly open; the rest heavily wooded.

One evening, after another frustrating weekend of looking at both well-cultivated and abandoned farms, we were on our way home, taking the back roads. Traveling along one concession road, we saw a small for-sale sign stuck to a tree. Strangely enough as soon as we stopped we both felt "this is it."

But what was it? It was late in the evening and we had no way of getting in touch with the owner or the agent. Furthermore, the sign looked years old. Was it possible that the land had been sold and the sign just left there? How many acres were there?

We spent a restless night, and I had a hard time containing myself until the real estate office opened. Monday morning at 9 o'clock on the dot, I dialed the number. The agent had almost forgotten the land I was describing. No, he did not have the listing any more, and could not tell me whether it had been sold or not. He gave me another number to call. After many more calls and frustrations, I finally tracked down the owner. Yes, he would meet us the next weekend and show us the land. So at least we now knew that it was still for sale. We also learned that it was a deserted farm, it had not been cultivated for over fifty years, and that it consisted of 132 acres, more or less. (We later learned that all farm deeds state a certain number of acres with the words "more or less" always tagged on to the description.)

Bright and early the next Saturday morning found us impatiently waiting for the owner at the designated spot. Nine-thirty was our appointment time, nine-thirty came and went, as did ten-thirty. Our hopes were at a low ebb at this point. Little did we know that this was to be only the first in a long series of waits and frustrations. The pace of country life is slow.

Finally the owner arrived. After introducing himself, he tried to describe the property — it stretched between two concession roads, was a mile deep, and a quarter of a mile wide, but we could not walk

16

through the whole length of the land because it was cut in half by a series of beaver dams. The front was partly cleared, as this was the site of the old homestead that had been cultivated many, many years ago. All that remained of the old homestead were the ruins of an old log cabin, now visible only as a pile of stones. The virgin forest of stately pines had been harvested in the late 1800s; the new growth was mainly red and white pine.

As we walked through the forest, we could see some remnants of the early settlers' labor — huge piles of stones and stone fences, oddly out of place in the middle of the bush. Finally we came to the beaver ponds which the forest engineers were busy repairing. Other wildlife moved about. We were delighted with our find.

The owner then took us around to the back of the property. Oh, what a delight! For some reason nature had decided to let the beaver ponds be the dividing line between the softwood and the hardwood forest. Thousands of sugar maples sprinkled with birch and oak covered this part of the land. How lucky can you get, I thought. But could we afford it? The farmer was a born salesman, not touching on the subject of price.When he finally did, the price was high.

However, I made a first, then a second offer. They were refused and I had already put an end to my dream, when I got an unexpected call from the owner. He asked me if I intended to cut down any trees. When he was convinced that I would leave as many trees standing as possible, he said he would accept my last offer, which was twenty per cent less than he had asked for originally. Believe me, a celebration took place in our house that night that you would not believe.

Not really knowing what we could grow on our land, we paid a visit to the local agricultural office. Most states and provinces have an excellent staff on duty at these offices to advise people in our situation, and we left with armfuls of free brochures and how-to books. Also, we took soil samples and submitted them for analysis.

SOIL CONDITIONS

In my travels around the country I have seen men forcing nature; only to find that anyone who tries to force nature is bound to fail. Most soils will grow a variety of fruits and vegetables. Soils do have a wide tolerance and broad adaptabilities, but certain crops have definite preferences and it is usually best to obey these rules. Stone fruits such as apples, pears, plums, and berries grow well in most soils, both in sandy and in clay loam. If you plan to specialize, make sure that your soil conditions and temperature range are suitable. Make it one winter's project to read everything you can find about your proposed specialty.

HAVE A MASTER PLAN

Build a temporary shelter as soon as possible, because, if your land is any distance away, too much time will be spent traveling back and forth. It may be a simple log cabin or, you may want to take temporary shelter in a small 8 x 10 foot trailer, as we did for the first three months.

Now is the time to put your ideas and dreams on paper — layouts of intended buildings, proposed roads and gardens, and a master plan of the whole property. If you do most of the work yourself, set out a schedule for all the different projects and by all means allow yourself lots of time to complete them. I found that all our projects took much more time than we had estimated.

If you plan to hire a man with a tractor or bulldozer to dig foundations or wells, remember that the country contractor is not the same as his brother in the city. When he says he will come next week, what he means is that he will come if he is not busy planting, hoeing, or harvesting somewhere else. Or, your project might interfere with his deer hunting trip or some other sporting event. He will come when he has nothing else to do. We found this out the hard way. Our farmer-contractor promised to come and dig our foundation in October. He did not show up until the middle of November. When reprimanded for this, he told us that he could not miss his hunting trip because he needed the meat for the winter!

CHAPTER 3

Inventory

Our first big undertaking was to take an inventory of everything on our woodlot. And I mean everything — wildlife, wildflowers, trees, bushes, stones, and grasses.

To do this we squared off the whole lot into approximate 100-foot squares. Then we started in one corner and worked our way through the whole area. It may seem an unnecessary task but, believe me, you can learn more about the soil and the condition of your land by taking an inventory than from a hundred soil samples from the government experimental station. Use your observations, together with the government's findings, and you will have a good idea of what you can grow and how you can benefit most from what is already there. Also, in a short time, you will get to know your land well as you spend many happy days working in the fresh air, enjoying the wonders of nature all around you.

On the acre of ground that would eventually become our front lawn, we found more edible plants than we could use in a lifetime; all there for the picking. In a corner near the old homestead there were about 50 fruit trees.

PLANTING AND PRUNING FRUIT TREES

The original orchard, in all likelihood, had been laid out properly, but, by self-seeding, hundreds of new trees had started to grow in all directions. We decided to keep the basic orchard and to take out some of the new trees and a few old ones which could not be brought back by pruning. It seemed a fairly simple chore — or so we thought. We soon found what a gigantic task it was to get the old orchard into working order. The biggest problem was to achieve the recommended planting distances as the trees were already well-rooted. The ideal planting

19

distance between apples (standard trees) is 30 to 35 feet, pears (standard trees) 18 to 22 feet, plums 18 to 22 feet, and cherries 27 to 33 feet. These distances are a general guide only. An old farmer and a neighbor of ours, Raymond Free, came over one day to see me when I was transplanting new trees. He took one look at me digging the holes for the new trees and said, "Don't mix the topsoil with the sub-soil." It is important to put the topsoil back in the holes first after the tree has been planted to allow the roots to grow out into the richer topsoil and give the tree a better start. He also advised me to dig the holes as I went, one by one, otherwise the soil would dry out before the trees were planted.

Before planting trim off broken, damaged, or dead root ends. Tramp the soil in firmly around the roots, but leave the last shovelful loose and leave a slight depression around the tree to catch run-off water the first summer. Position the tree with the lowest limb toward the prevailing wind and lean the tree slightly in the same direction, so that it will stand straight when the orchard is established.

It is also important to place guards around each tree at planting time to protect the young trees from mice and rabbits. The guards should be sunk 2 to 3 inches below ground level to hold them firmly and to discourage mice.

One of the hardest jobs, but one that must be done, is to prune the newly planted tree. It is hard because the tree looks like a tree before planting, whereas after you are through pruning you end up with a stick standing in the ground. However, it must be done to lessen loss of water, to mitigate adverse wind effects, and to compensate for much of the root system lost when the tree was lifted out of the nursery row.

If you do not know how to prune large, growing trees, the best thing to do is get a professional to do the first pruning and observe carefully how he does it. The next time you will be able to do it yourself.

EDIBLE FRUITS, BERRIES, WEEDS, AND GRASSES

APPLES Learn how to store your apples properly. Commercially, apples are usually stored in a temperature-and-humidity controlled atmosphere. The composition of the air allows the apples to "sleep" or respire as slowly as possible in order to give them the appearance of freshly picked fruit all year round.

RASPBERRIES Growing wild under the old apples were stands of wild raspberries. In some places they were so dense that we could not walk through the stands. First, we cut out the old canes that had died after bearing fruit. While cleaning out the old canes, we also removed all the small, weak suckers and burned both the old canes and the suckers, because they can become disease carriers.

WILD CURRANTS Intertwined with the raspberry stands were wild currant bushes. Here again we pruned out the old canes. They should be pruned when they are dormant; ideally in January or February. Currants produce best on one-year-old wood. Strong one-year-old shoots, or two-year-old shoots with an abundance of strong one-year-old wood, are the most productive.

We found that propagation of the currant bushes was easy. We cut off 6 to 8 inches in the late fall from that season's wood, the bottom cut just below a bud, and the top cut about one-half an inch above a bud. The cuttings were set about 6 inches apart in well-drained soil at such a depth that one or two buds extended out of the soil. We then mulched with straw. In a year's time, these plants were just right for planting. Even cultivated plants can be propagated in this manner, thus cutting costs.

WILD STRAWBERRIES In open places around the apple trees we found an abundance of wild strawberries. The berries of the wild plants are not as large as those from cultivated plants, but their fragrance and flavor more than make up for the small size.

We found that keeping weeds out as much as possible, then watering with rainwater spiked with cow manure resulted in much larger berries. We prepare the "brew," as my wife calls it, by collecting rainwater in an old tub which has 3 to 4 forkfuls of manure added to it. This stands for a week or so before use. We add manure about once a month or so.

GOLDENROD There is a lot of goldenrod growing around the open spaces on the homestead. In the fall we collect the flowers for making tea during the winter months. Many people are allergic to the pollen but anyone can drink the tea without bad effects.

The tea is a stimulant, in the same sense as ordinary tea. Some people use it to relieve nausea, pain in the stomach or bowels, and believe it dissolves gas in the stomach.

DANDELION This plant was, of course, everywhere, and was a welcome addition to our green salads in the early spring and summer. The roots can be dried in the sun to make an excellent coffee substitute.

Dandelions contain a large amount of vitamins A and E (twenty-five times more vitamin A than an equal amount of orange juice and 50 times more than asparagus). The plant also contains large amounts of calcium, chlorine, magnesium, potassium, and silica. Because of its

21

mineral salt content it is helpful in even severe illnesses such as pulmonary tuberculosis and some genital-urinary conditions.

CHICKWEED   This weed was abundant around our fence line. It is excellent raw in a green salad early in the spring; later in the summer and fall it is better cooked. The taste is not unlike that of okra.

The uses of chickweed are varied, as it contains mineral salts and possesses an unidentified healing property which offers relief for many skin and eye problems and some rheumatic ailments.

WILD ASPARAGUS   Wild asparagus tips are used in the same way as cultivated asparagus. The only difference is in the size; the wild tips are smaller but make up for it by being much tastier. They appear early in the spring.

This wild plant has been used as a heart sedative, and it is credited with preventing a build-up of kidney stones.

BLACK MUSTARD   It grows on dry, sandy soil and is easily identified by its bright yellow flowers. Early in the spring young mustard plants are tasty either raw in a salad or cooked as a vegetable in a stew or soup.

As a cold remedy this plant has a long-standing reputation via the mustard plaster to loosen mucus in the lungs. It still works. Indians often used it as a cold preventative in wet weather by adding a heaping tablespoonful of the mustard powder to warm water in a large bowl. They then soaked their feet in this mixture, stirring it from time to time and adding more hot water.

COMMON PLANTAIN   Wherever there is an open spot along a gravel road or a stream bank, you will find this plant. We use it most often in green salads, but it is excellent also as a substitute for spinach. When lightly steamed, cut up into small pieces, and added to a white sauce, it is a dish fit for a king.

Plantain is used to stop bleeding from cuts and sores; the juice from the leaves takes the pain from and helps heal burns and scalds, also lessens the irritation from insect or spider bites, and wasp or bee stings. Some people find it even helps to remove the irritation from poison ivy infections.

EVENING PRIMROSE   Found in dry, sandy soil, this flower is familiar to most people because of the flowers, which open at dusk. The flowers are four-petaled, delicate, and pale yellow in color. After being peeled, the leaves can be used in a green salad, but the best way to use this plant is to dig up the roots, wash, and boil them as carrots, then cook in a stew or as a vegetable.

GREAT BURDOCK This very common plant has a multitude of uses in the kitchen. The young roots peeled and sliced make an unusually good potherb and the young shoots are tasty either eaten raw or in a salad. Later in the summer the leaves can be cooked like spinach. (The taste is not unlike that of spinach.)

It promotes sweating and urination, and is very cleansing for impure blood. Many rheumatism and gout sufferers claim it has soothing properties.

LAMB'S QUARTERS OR PIGWEED This plant was one of the first greens the early settlers had after a long winter without fresh green vegetables. In the early spring the whole plant can be put in a salad or boiled and chopped and served in a sauce. The seeds were often used by the Indians for making cereal or ground into meal to make bread and biscuits. Seeds in bread or biscuits add a pumpernickel taste.

MILKWEED This plant stands from 2 to 5-feet tall and is easy to recognize by its large leaves, placed opposite each other, and by its milky juice. The young shoots of the milkweed, washed and cut into small pieces, make a good potherb. Later in the summer the small seed pods can be boiled whole and eaten as a vegetable. In the fall I like to remove the seeds, fill the pods with meat, and cook them like a cabbage roll.

When the green plant is bruised and applied externally, it is a good healing agent for sores and ulcers. The roots, when bruised and put into gin, are reputed to be good for coughs, asthma, and rheumatism.

MINT This plant is characterized by square stems, opposite simple leaves, small purple or white flowers, and a fragrant smell. You cannot miss the refreshing aroma of these plants when you come upon a mint patch. The leaves can either be eaten raw or in a salad. It is especially good for flavoring all varieties of meat.

Yerbabuena (the Spanish name for mint tea) is claimed to be the best thing in the world for restoring sexual vigor.

FERN Both Ostrich and Bracken fern produce sterile fronds which form circular clumps. The part to pick is the fiddlehead, before it reaches a height of 5 to 6 inches and is still curly and rust-colored. Fiddleheads are edible just as they are — simply clean and eat. Boiled in salted water and served with drippings from the frying pan, they are just out of this world.

The rust covering the fronds is an excellent agent for removing poison ivy or poison oak oil from the skin.

PURSLANE   Purslane was a common potherb in Persia and is mentioned in 2000-year-old manuscripts. Its succulent branches hug the ground and its leaves are broad at the tips, tapering towards the base. The seed capsules contain many thousands of flat, oval, black seeds. The juicy, slightly sour stems and leaves are delightful when eaten raw, and are thirst quenching. Purslane was often used by the Indians and the early settlers either as a green or pickled in vinegar.

Many healing properties are claimed for this plant, but I have had no first-hand experience with it. Made as a tea it is known to be helpful for many blood disorders. It has a high Vitamin C and iron content.

SHEEP SORREL   This plant is very common. It is also known as sourgrass. The leaves are arrowhead shaped and distinctly sour-tasting. Sheep sorrel was used by early settlers in soups, salads, and for making drinks.

A poultice made out of the crushed leaves has a cooling and soothing effect. It is therefore often applied to tumors and inflammations.

STINGING NETTLE   This plant is easy to identify. All you have to do is give the leaves a swat with the back of your hand, which will cause a painful stinging sensation to the skin.

Nettle leaves should be gathered in the early spring when they first appear. First, dip the leaves in boiling water to remove the small hairs that cause the burning sensation. When boiled, very young nettle shoots resemble bean sprouts in flavor and texture. Blanched young shoots can be used in green salads and are particularly good in soup.

The nettle is rich in mineral salts and vitamins. It is one of my favorite remedies for curing a chill developing into a cold, in which case I use it as a tea. The nettle is also helpful and safe for women on a slimming diet, as it eliminates superfluous liquid in the body. The leaves of the nettle are used to stop bleeding, even from severe wounds and the juice is sometimes used as a natural hair tonic. What more can you ask from so common a plant?

When pounded, fine fibers can be extracted from the stem. These can be used as fishlines if one is really desperate.

THISTLE   Despite its unlikely appearance as an edible plant, the thistle was used by the Greeks and Romans as a potherb.

Remove the leaves and cut off the tips that hold the sharp marginal prickles. The leaves can be eaten either raw or cooked, as can the stalks after the tough skin has been removed.

According to some European sources, the stems, after the skin has been removed can be made into wine; in fact, a wine with a splendid tonic quality.

24

WATERCRESS   This succulent plant which grows in slow-moving water is an excellent source of vitamin C. It is delicious in a green salad, but it can also be boiled and used in a stew.

It is said to be helpful for cleansing the blood, purifying the liver, and for dissolving bladder stones. It has also been used in treating skin ailments.

WINTERGREEN   This low shrub, barely 6 inches tall, is found in rocky or dry, sandy loam. The creeping stems are half hidden by foliage which grows reddish branches bearing ovate, glossy, leathery leaves. The fruit is bright scarlet berries which can either be eaten raw or made into a wonderful jam. The leaves can be used for a tea, to flavor stews, or added to roasts.

The oil, when extracted from the leaves and mixed with maple syrup, makes a deliciously different maple candy.

Wintergreen is used as a stimulant, an antiseptic, to cure rheumatism, and help menstrual troubles and chronic diarrhea.

YELLOW CLOVER   Even small children can recognize clover. We all have at one time or another looked for a lucky four-leaf clover, but the soft, green leaves are usually arranged in threes. The flowers can be bright yellow, purple, or plain white. Clover can be eaten raw after it has been dipped in salted water or it can be cut up and added to a salad. The flowers are a good source of nectar, as the honey bee well knows.

Clover can be made into a tea which seems to have unusual cleansing and healing properties. The red and purple clovers have even been credited with healing certain forms of cancer.

ARROWHEAD   This plant can usually be found growing around beaver dams. Wapato, as the Indians called it, was widely used by them and they often raided muskrat houses in the fall to gather enough tubers to last the winter. Settlers soon discovered how delicious this plant was, and often used it as a substitute for potatoes. The tubers *can* be eaten raw, but they taste much better when cooked.

BULRUSH AND CATTAIL   These plants grow around the shores of streams and ponds. The young shoots can be eaten raw or mixed in a salad. The shoots can be gathered all year around. When we cleared our land, we piled branches and brush on top of the dried-out plants sticking through the ice and put fire to the brush. The heat from the fire melted the ice and we had easy access to the green shoots. When the roots or bulbs are scraped and boiled they taste very much like potatoes. They are, however, full of fibers. I much prefer to boil the roots into a heavy gruel and then let the water evaporate. Sift what remains through a flour sifter to remove all the fibers. This leaves a fine flour, excellent for baking bread and cakes.

WILD ONION   In the hardwood bush early in the spring we can collect all the onions we need for most of the summer. Wild onion leaves are broad and elliptical; they disappear before the flowers emerge. The bulb and the stem are excellent either eaten raw or prepared as one would a domestic onion.

A thick syrup (made by boiling down the juice of the wild onion) is used to curb laryngitis, coughs, and bronchitis. A thick poultice can be made by mixing the syrup with flour to treat eczema and inflammations.

BEARBERRY   This trailing, evergreen ground cover with its hard red berries and small, shiny dark green leaves is called kinnickinnick by the Indians and is used instead of cranberry sauce in the Scandinavian countries. For a mid-winter feast of fresh berries, pick them when they are bright red and place in an empty bottle with a screw top. Only whole berries should be used. Fill the bottle as full as you can with berries, then fill with distilled water, secure top, and store in a cold but not freezing place. Take out at Christmas. Drain off the water, sprinkle with sugar and serve. They will taste quite fresh. The shiny small leaves, dried, are an excellent substitute for pipe tobacco.

WILD RICE   In the lower beaver dam we have a small patch of wild rice. This plume-topped grass, which grows from 4 to 6 feet tall, is getting scarce around this part of the country. The patch we have is not enough at the present time to harvest, but with a little care we should have enough for our own use. If not, at least the ducks will love it and it will attract wild fowl which otherwise would not eat or nest at our pond.

WILD ROSE   Some 35 or more varieties of wild rose are found in the United States and Canada. We have counted eight different varieties of wild rose and at least four different cultivated roses that have gone wild. The fruit from the rose hip is one of Mother Nature's ways to capture vitamins. The rose hip has 50 times more vitamin C than an orange, by volume. The small stones in the fruit, if crushed and added to the juice extracted from the hip, hold large amounts of vitamin E, A, and B_1.

Some doctors say the perfume of roses contains a quality which relieves worry, lessens anxiety, and promotes longevity. A tea made from the dried petals is said to restore health to the eyes and to increase one's ability to see in the dark. It is said that the soldiers of

Alexander the Great's army often used this tea to obtain better sight at night, although, of course, they had no knowledge of the effect of Vitamin A on eyesight.

TREES

PRICKLY ASH   Often called the Toothache Tree, this is a small tree or bush growing from 4 to 8 feet high with an abundance of prickles. I remember the first spring on the homestead when I first came in contact with this bush as I was trying to clear a path for our vegetable garden. After I had worked all morning clearing bush my wife took a horrified look at me and said "Have you been in a fight with a cat?" My face had been cut almost to ribbons by the very sharp prickles which are as sharp as a surgeon's knife and when a branch from the bushes hits your face and makes a minute cut you hardly feel it. What good comes from a tree so dangerous? Early in the spring, a small green flower appears and after the flower has disappeared a small oval capsule forms; each capsule holds an oval black seed. This seed can be harvested, ground into a powder, and used in small quantities as a remedy for toothache, or as a treatment for chronic rheumatism.

WILD CHERRY   Black, rum, and pin cherries grow in abundance on our property and of course the fruit is used for jams and jellies if we are able to collect them before the birds get them all. We found that a simple way to scare off the birds was to cut thick aluminum foil into 2-inch strips and tie them to a branch of the tree by means of a string through a hole in one end. The wind moves the foil, causing a rustling noise and continuous flashes of light, which frightens birds.

STAG SUMACH   This tree or bush is easily recognized by its stout, velvety twigs, which resemble deer antlers in velvet. Later in the fall the torch-like pinnacle of fruit and bright crimson leaves leave no doubt of the identification. We usually harvest the crimson berries late in the fall and dry them for use during the winter months as an excellent substitute for lemonade, since the berries have a tart lemon-like taste.

A poultice made of the crushed leaves and flowers applied to irritated skin ulcers or old sores seems to have a healing effect. A gargle made of the crushed berries and leaves in a small amount of water is a good old-fashioned remedy for sore throats.

BLACK BIRCH   This tree is easily identified by its reddish brown bark, which has the aroma of wintergreen. The leaves are dull green on the upperside and pale green on the underside — the shape of the typical betula family. The bark dried and finely ground and mixed into home-made soup adds an aromatic wintergreen smell.

HEMLOCK This makes a medium good building material, as the trunk is usually straight but very tapered. It should be used in places where it is protected from wetness. Since hemlock is very susceptible to decay it is usually difficult to find completely sound wood. However, a very good tea can be made from the young hemlock needles.

Oil can be extracted from the bark of the hemlock tree by finely grinding the bark, then boiling it in water and skimming off the oil. The oil is thought to be useful when applied externally to treat rheumatism and lumbago.

essanders

RED PINE

RED PINE This stately tree can be identified by the rough bark and the 3-cluster needles. One of the best woods for construction of log buildings, these trees can reach a height of up to 150 feet. They usually grow straight.

WHITE PINE   Also a stately tree with a smoother bark than the red pine, the white pine has leaves or needles placed in clusters of five. If you have difficulty remembering which is which, here is a simple rule. *Red* has 3 letters, *white* has 5 letters, the same number of needles as letters in its name.

GBSanders

WHITE PINE

RED CEDAR   This is one of North America's most durable woods. It can stand damp and dry rot better than any other wood I know.

If you can get big enough trees, they are ideal for log-building. You may have difficulty getting them if there are none growing on your land, because they are in great demand as hydro and telephone poles. But if you can build a house of red cedar, you will have an aromatic, durable building. It is also excellent wood for making shingles or shakes.

29

BLACK SPRUCE   One of the most-used building materials, black spruce usually grows straight and is a relatively soft wood, easy to drive nails into without splitting. This tree lends itself to the cutting of planks either by hand-sawing or by using a circular saw.

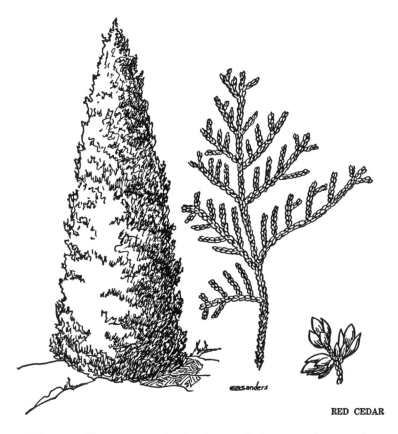

RED CEDAR

SUGAR MAPLE   No one can mistake the maple for any other tree in our bush. The maples are deciduous trees with opposite, simple, or compound, variably lobed leaves, and a smooth bark. The wood from the maple lends itself to furniture making and paneling.

Most sought after is the sap which is made into syrup and sugar. This stately tree yields from 3 to 6 pounds of sap every year. The sap was one of the Indian's main sources of sweetening. The use of the maple tree as a food source was more than likely one of the greatest gifts from the Indians to the white man when he first came to America.

OAK   A beautiful tree but, unfortunately, due to slow growing and very heavy harvesting, not too many of these trees are to be seen in our bush. The wood is very hard and therefore excellent for paneling and for making floors. Oak was widely used in furniture-making by the early settlers.

BLACK SPRUCE

BASSWOOD This tree is easily recognized by its large heart-shaped leaves. The wood itself was often used for making bowls and other household items such as spoons and spatulas. It was also a favorite for maple sugar moulds or for carvings, as this soft wood hardly ever chips or splinters.

WHITE ASH Early settlers used it for making the bodies of planes and other tools because its smooth tight grain, after a little use, could be polished to a high degree.

The bark from the white ash, finely ground and burned, was used by the early settlers much as we use Aspirin tablets today.

31

WHITE BIRCH Also called canoe birch because of its very pliable bark, this was often used by the Indians to cover their canoes and as material for pots and pans before the white man introduced cast-iron utensils. Today it is used mainly for furniture making or paneling.

SUGAR MAPLE

ASPEN POPLAR Quivering aspen is another and most appropriate name for this tree because in the slightest breeze, its small rounded leaves, with their lively quivering motion, make it stand out. The stems of the leaves, while comparatively broad, are paper thin and act as a hinge, causing the quivering movement of the leaves. The Cree Indians have another explanation. Their story is that when the Great Magician created the trees he protected the white birch from the furor of the Thunder God. The aspen tree was jealous of this protection and tried to copy the structure of the leaves and stem of the white birch but could not quite make it. Ever since then, the aspen has lived in fear that the Great Magician would discover the fraud; hence its leaves always quiver.

The wood is very good for fuel and, as it is straight and splits easily, it was used by the early settlers for making wooden pegs and pins for wooden rakes.

WHITE OAK

BUTTERNUT   This is a close relative of the black walnut and is often confused with it. It is easy to identify by its grayish bark and the thin husks which enclose the nuts.

In the fall nuts can be collected and put away to dry, ready to use about Christmastime. The wood is used for furniture and resembles that of black walnut but is lighter in color.

33

YELLOW BIRCH   This tree is the most important timber tree of all our hardwoods. It is a much larger tree than the white birch, sometimes reaching a height of 100 feet or more. Its bark is papery but does not tear off like that of the white birch.

The bark is yellow or straw-colored, hence its name. The wood is strong and heavy and has a pleasing reddish color. It is an excellent wood for flooring, furniture, and interior trim.

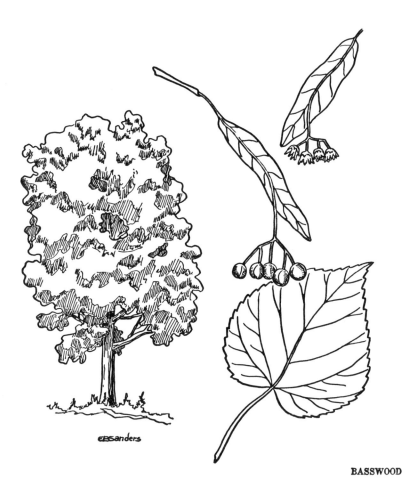

BASSWOOD

IRONWOOD   A comparatively small tree, ironwood is found mixed with beech, maple, ash, and elm. The name ironwood is most appropriate because of its hard, tough nature. It was at one time widely used for tools, wagon parts, and for hinges in the old cabins.

34

AMERICAN ELM Few trees have been more loved than the American Elm. Unfortunately, in recent years they have become infected with Dutch Elm Disease which has killed almost all elms in North America. The wood, strong and tough, was used for making furniture, casks, barrels, baskets, and cheese boxes.

EBSanders

WHITE ASH

SASSAFRAS Unlike most trees, this has three different forms of leaves on the same tree. It is best known by the strong, pleasing taste and smell of its bark, twigs, and roots. It grows to a height of 30 to 40 feet. The bark is usually boiled in hot water and the oil is skimmed off and used for flavoring and perfume. The bark, finely ground, can be made into a tea.

Medically the tea has been used as a stimulant in the treatment of rheumatism, kidney trouble, and corrosive poisons; as a poultice it can be placed on old sores and inflammations of the skin.

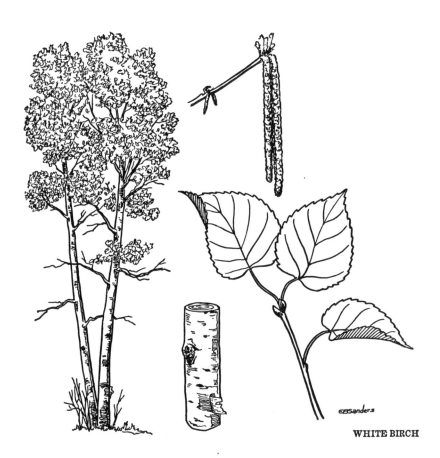

WHITE BIRCH

ANIMALS

WHITE-TAILED DEER   The only cloven-hoofed animal on our homestead is the White-Tailed Deer. This deer is the smallest of its family. The body is gray or grayish brown, the underparts, including the chest and the inside of the legs and underside of the tail, are white. Antlers project upward and outward from the head with individual tines growing from the main antler beam.

As the White-Tailed buck is polygamous and will breed with as many does as he encounters during the breeding season, we are careful only to kill a buck when we have several of them.

The deer feed primarily on browse species such as aspen, choke-cherry, and dogwood but also eat berries and some grasses and forbs. Controlled hunting is a must to maintain a healthy herd. As the deer has no natural predator in our area, overcrowding and starvation will occur if too large a herd is allowed to develop. To maintain a proper balance we usually kill one or two annually.

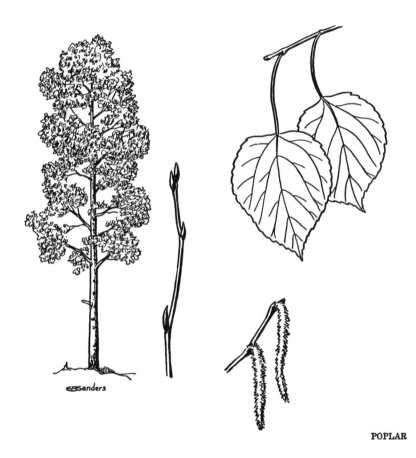

POPLAR

BEAVER The beaver is a heavy-set animal with webbed feet and prominent incisor teeth. Its greatest peculiarity is a flat, paddle-shaped tail which is bare of fur and somewhat scaly. Its color varies from a light to a very dark brown; some specimens being almost black. The beaver generally mates for life and produces a litter of about four annually.

Here again it pays to keep close tabs on the number of animals, so that overcrowding does not occur. Careful trapping may be necessary

37

to keep the number of animals down so that the remaining ones have enough food to live. Beavers will move away to find more food and leave an empty pond which soon will be without fish and other animals or birds as the beaver dam deteriorates. The food much preferred by this industrious animal is the aspen and other small deciduous trees and branches.

The beaver constructs a dam to keep the water in the pond at a level which makes it easy to float the trees he cuts and to make sure that the openings of the beaver house are not above water level.

MUSKRAT   A muskrat family has moved into our beaver pond, much to our delight. This amphibious rodent, about four times the size of the ordinary rat, with short legs and partly webbed strong hind feet has a long, bare, vertical, and flattened tail, feeding on vegetable matter and some fish, clams, and young birds.

RED SQUIRREL   This small animal is chiefly a tree dweller and is distinguished by red coloration and a large bushy tail nearly as long as the head and body. Mating generally takes place in late March or early April and 4 to 6 young are born in late May. The meat is dark in color and very tasty, and its hide is also very useful. It is wise to keep the number of squirrels down as they feed on birds' eggs and young birds.

RED FOX   This shy animal of the dog family is not seen very often but you can, during the winter, see his tracks and the occasional spot where an unwary grouse has been killed.

If you plan to keep chickens, keep an eye on the fox family, but as they also feed on rodents, they are an asset to your bush.

SKUNK   This stinker is easily identified by its sturdy body, large bushy tail, and thick, long, glossy black fur with a narrow white stripe running from snout to crown, and usually two white stripes extending from the back of its head to the root of its tail. Their diet consists mainly of mice, frogs, grasshoppers, and other assorted insects, but they have been known to consume domestic and other birds. Do not be surprised to find them in the chicken coop enjoying the freshly laid eggs.

JACK RABBIT AND COTTONTAIL RABBIT   Both species are around our homestead. The jack rabbit, the largest of the hares or rabbits, measures up to 30 inches in length and weighs up to 20 pounds. They are brownish gray in summer and pale gray in the winter; the back of the ears are white with black tips. Rabbits feed mainly on a wide range of vegetables, clover, wild grasses, grains, and buds. With rabbits around your homestead you are better to have your vegetable garden fenced in with chicken wire, and make sure before winter comes that you put wire mesh around your small newly planted fruit trees as they like to chew the bark of small trees and branches. Remember to cover the trees well up the trunk because, after several snowfalls, rabbits will be able to reach much higher than you think.

The cottontail, although smaller than the jack rabbit, can do as much damage to the garden and fruit trees. Both species are excellent eating; in fact, an old Scandinavian custom is to have rabbit on the Christmas table.

BIRDS

SPRUCE GROUSE   These birds are plentiful in our thick stands of pine and spruce. A small, very dark grouse, the male's back and wings are dusky brown to dusky blue and each feather is finely barred with black. The face is black, with a white line behind each eye and a scarlet comb above, the throat is black, sometimes marked with white. The rest of the bird is black with white bars.

The spruce grouse nests on the ground in a nest made out of leaves and grasses placed under the low-hanging branches of a spruce tree. The eggs, usually 8 to 10 but sometimes as many as 16, are usually light brown, beautifully marked with dark brown.

When hunting spruce grouse, bear in mind their defense tactic. They usually flutter into the branches of a tight-branched conifer when you approach and then depend on their protective coloration and immobility to make them inconspicuous. They will let you so close you can almost touch them, and then will disappear. That is why they are called Fool's Hen.

RUFFED GROUSE   Walking through bush in the spring you often hear a sound that resembles the muffled roll of a drum. This is the male Ruffed Grouse putting on a show to attract the female. You will hear him long before you see him. The best way to approach is to sneak up while he is drumming, stopping when he stops. Eventually you will see the bird. The head, crested with a ruff of glossy black feathers on each side of the neck, and a fairly long tail with a black band near the tip, are the most distinguishing marks. They also nest on the ground, but, unlike the spruce grouse, select a fairly open spot usually near or under a fallen log or root. The eggs, usually 8 to 14, are buff-colored and unspotted.

RING-NECKED PHEASANT   What is more exciting than to see a large pheasant lifting in front of a bird dog? This bird is bright and beautifully colored with iridescent purple on the head or neck, iridescent bronze and black on the body, usually a white ring around the neck, and a multicolored, long tail. This is the plumage of the male ring-necked pheasant. It is found close to clearings with plenty of tight cover, in tangled willows, in rose bushes, or in tall grass or weeds along streams or ditches. The meat is semi-dark and sweet.

HUNGARIAN PARTRIDGE   If when walking through the bush the stillness is suddenly broken by the deafening chatter of a fast-flying bird emerging from the bush, one has probably disturbed a Hungarian partridge. This bird certainly puts the hunter to a test. Its characteristic sudden flight usually unnerves the hunter and by the time he has recovered, the bird is long gone. The Hungarian partridge is a small, brownish bird. It has a light brown face and throat, usually some evidence of a chestnut horseshoe on the lower breast, and, in flight, the chestnut tail feathers are obvious. Its flesh is highly prized but the bird rarely weights more than 15 to 20 ounces.

CANADA GOOSE   We are in the middle of the Atlantic flyway and occasionally have flocks of Canada Geese feeding on the wild rice on our pond during the fall migration. This stately bird has white cheek patches on a black head, its back and wings are grayish brown with lighter feather edging. The abdomen and upper and lower tail are white, the beak, neck, tail, and legs are black. Its meat has often substituted for turkey on our Christmas table.

DUCKS   On our pond we have many species of ducks nesting in harmony with our domestic ducks. We have, as permanent guests, Mallards, Blacks, Pintail, Widgeon, and Teals.

The dark, delightful-tasting meat of ducks is always welcome on our dinner table.

FISH

RAINBOW TROUT   In the stream running through our property, rainbow trout are plentiful. There are as many ways to catch rainbow as there are fishermen. All kinds of baits and lures can be used; from trolling spoons to frozen lumps of vaseline. Personally, I like my fly-casting outfit best, particularly in fast-running water late in the evening when the fish are feeding on nymphs and duns.

YELLOW PERCH   Can you think of anything more soothing and relaxing during a late summer evening than to sit on the bank of a beaver dam holding a basswood pole and fishing for perch? Perch provide fast action; their appetite makes up for what they lack in fighting qualities. Remember to dangle your bait about a foot off the bottom.

COMMON SUCKER   Early in the spring just after the ice has left, suckers come up our stream to spawn. They are usually so thick that they can be harvested with bare hands. "But what in the world are you going to use them for?" my neighbor questioned, "You can't eat them." Oh yes we can. As a matter of fact, suckers, if caught early in the spring when the water is still cold, then smoked, make delightful eating. How often have you been served mullet in a restaurant? Did you know that mullet is the commercial trade name for sucker flesh?

CRAWFISH   or crayfish as it is also called, is a small lobster-like crustacean that we have in abundance in our pond. When I talk about eating this little fish, people usually assume that there is very little flesh on it. Not so. We have taken crawfish from our pond that were 3 to 4 inches long, measured from head to the end of the tail, disregarding the claws. In the Scandinavian countries it is illegal to keep crawfish under 3¾ inches long. This is an excellent practice, as it builds up a reserve of good stock. People usually use crawfish as bait for bass or pike, but if you leave them in the pond as we do, you can feast on them in late fall.

EEL   People often have an aversion to this fat and delightful fish, perhaps because it looks like a snake. But on our table freshly caught and smoked eel is a delicacy at any time. Cooked with dill and served cold it is greatly enjoyed as long as people are not told what they are eating.

CHAPTER 4

Tall Trees Falling

LOG CABINS

Building a log house requires as much planning as any other building. The first step is to acquire a good set of blueprints from someone familiar with this kind of construction. It seems that people think of the log house as a cabin or shanty built by the settler as a temporary housing project, but this is not so. True enough, in many instances, a small log cabin was first erected on the homestead to house the settler and his family during the first year or so until he had time to build a more permanent building.

If you are fortunate enough to have tall timber on your land, this, more than likely, will be what you will use to build your own home. There are two methods of construction. The oldest method uses hand-hewn logs piled on top of each other with intricate notches in the corners and around window and door openings. The other, much newer method, uses timber as a frame, covering the frame outside and inside with hand-sawn boards or planks. In either case you need good, long, solid timber as building material.

SELECTING THE RIGHT TREE

Selecting the right trees is an art in itself and here are some guidelines to follow. Being the son of a district forester in whose family the same forestry district has been handed down from father to son since 1163, I was, at an early age, trained to evaluate and judge trees standing in the forest. The first consideration is the conservation of the wood lot. Take great care when you select the trees to be cut that the woods surrounding your building site will not be depleted of trees.

The size of trees to be marked for cutting depends largely on the size of the building you intend to erect. The logs have to be suitable to

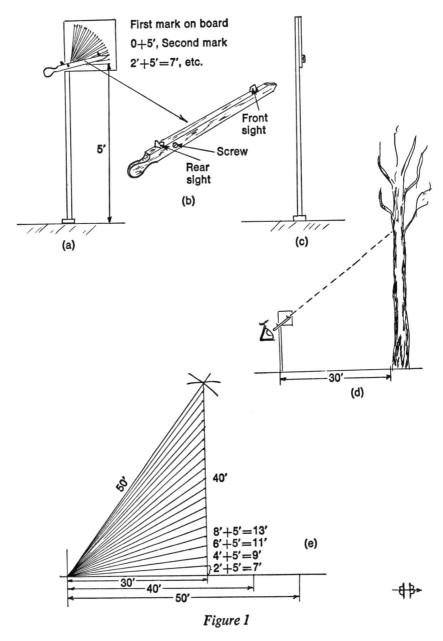

First mark on board
0+5', Second mark
2'+5'=7', etc.

5'

(a)

Front
sight

Screw

Rear
sight

(b)

(c)

30'

(d)

50'

40'

8'+5'=13'
6'+5'=11'
4'+5'=9'
2'+5'=7'

(e)

30'
40'
50'

Figure 1

Diagrams illustrate how to measure the height of a tree. (a) complete measuring device; (b) sighting stick; (c) side view; (d) measuring device in operation; (e) measuring scale.

44

the building; a small building should have smaller logs — large buildings require larger ones. If the building is to be about 20 x 20 feet square, then 10 to 12-inch logs should be used. A 30-foot square building should have 14 to 16-inch timber. (The measurement is the diameter of a standing tree taken at breast height.)

The tree should be straight, without too much taper, and have no split or crotch in it. The best way to evaluate a tree is to stand back and sight up from different angles, then move in close to the trunk and size it up along the trunk. Do not get discouraged if you have a hard time finding perfectly straight trees, because they are few and far between. There are few things I admire more than a good axeman and, believe me, to get a good looking building from crooked trees you have to be good with an axe.

I have found that the biggest problem the beginner has to contend with is judging the height of a tree. An easy way to find out is to make a sighting post: On a flat piece of ground lay out two straight lines so they form a right angle (the triangle-measuring method) the sides to be 3 and 4 and the hypotenuse 5. Cut a pole long enough to reach to your eye level. Nail a piece of plywood or any other flat surface on which you can mark the height on the top of your pole. Fasten on one end of this flat surface a sighting device which can be moved up and down to line up the front and rear sights. (Fig. 1)

Measure 30 feet along one of the lines and then place your sighting device flat on the ground with the base where the two lines meet. Now, along the other line, set off measurements at 5-foot intervals. Drive a pole or stick in the ground where the two lines meet and, using a string, move the loose end of the string along the measured line, taking care that you mark off on the board each 5-foot distance. When using this tool, step away 30 feet from the tree you are measuring, sight along the sighting device, and move it until you have reached the height of the tree where you must cut it. Read off the height on the flat surface and you now know the length of the timber you are getting. (Fig. 1)

Before you mark the tree, take into consideration where it can be felled to the best advantage for branching and skidding. You want the tree to fall in an open spot where there is less chance of it becoming hung up in other trees.

Logs are best cut in the winter when the sap is down in the tree since they are a great deal lighter then. Skidding the tree out from the bush is much easier on snow, with much less mechanical damage to the timber. (I like to do my cutting in late fall before the snow comes as this gives me a better footing and it is easier to work on bare ground, but I usually leave the skidding until after the snow has fallen.)

Illustrated above is the correct way to haul and stack logs.

I prefer to leave the bark on until the logs are at the building site, where they are laid on a bed of short timber, only one layer on each set of cross timbers. Try to level the cross timber as best you can, otherwise the timber will take the shape of the log pile, and a perfectly straight piece will end up crooked in the spring. A lot of people have the idea that the longer you season the timber the better it will be as a building material. That is not so. You are overlooking the fact that timber will set as it dries and it is better to have the logs set in the building where they are going to stay. Do not hurry, the more careful you are in piling the timber, the easier it will be to bark and hew in the spring. Sort the logs as you bring them from the bush. I usually have two piles of logs, long ones for the sides and shorter ones for the ends.

HOW TO FELL TREES

How many people know how to fell a tree properly? Our neighbor, Jack Macoun tells the story about his grandfather and great-uncle, the well-known botanist, John Macoun, who came to this country as settlers and had to clear the land for their farm. Their acreage was covered with virgin pine with butt ends up to 3 feet and more. They had never seen trees that big in their homeland in Scotland and they started to cut all around one with their axes. When asked which way the tree was going to fall, they both answered, "How should we know, we are not bloody prophets." They were very surprised to learn that they could indeed influence the outcome, simply by inflicting the initial cuts in the proper way.

Before you make that initial cut take a good look at how the tree is leaning or you might have to take the precaution of using wedges to help it go the way you want it to. The initial cut or the undercut as it is called, should be placed in the side where you want the tree to fall. Then, on the opposite side, about 2 to 3 inches above the undercut, start the backcut. Put a wedge in on the side opposite the fall you desire, and hammer it in.

Here are a few safety rules you should remember:

1. Check your getaway path, in other words a clear trail to a safe place. Always make it to one side and behind the stump, in respect to the direction of fall.
2. Remember that the butt of the tree can kick back and traverse several feet up in the air.
3. Always wear a safety hat. Dry branches may be dislodged when the tree starts to fall; even fresh branches can ricochet.

4. If the saw binds as the tree starts to go, leave it in the cut and stand back. Most of the time no harm comes to the saw, but even if the saw breaks it is better to have a broken saw than a broken back.
5. Be extremely careful when dislodging a hung-up tree. Never try to cut down the tree that is holding the partly downed tree. Use your tractor (or horses) and a small chain which will break easily in case of undue stress. If you use too strong a chain you might find yourself pulled under the tree when it comes down.

LOCATION OF BUILDINGS

Location is vitally important. No clearing of land should take place before you have made up your mind about your building site.

Here are a few points to take into consideration before you make your selection. First of all, is there water nearby or is it possible to dig a well by hand or get a well-drilling rig into the place? Water is something you will need a lot of, both during construction and after. The site should be on high ground to make drainage from the foundation, as well as from the septic-tank system, easier. Take a soil sample of the ground nearby and have your local Sanitation Officer test it to find if the soil is suitable for good drainage.

High ground also provides a breeze during the spring and summer months and helps keep away bugs of all kinds. You will also appreciate a light breeze during the hot nights in summer. Naturally, the view is something else to take into consideration. After all these things have been taken into account, start clearing the ground. If at all possible this should be done by hand because the surrounding trees and vegetation will suffer much less damage if you can do it this way. If you have to hire a back-hoe, be prepared to pay for some extra time so that the operator can go around trees and vegetation. (You will appreciate them later on when you start to landscape around the buildings.)

TOOLS

You will require a certain number of tools. The early settlers were said to have carried their whole tool chest on their backs, and this was true. Start with a good-quality axe (I prefer the Hudson Bay, one-bitted type). Some people prefer the double-bitted axe, but I have never got used to it. You will need one or two broad axes, a light one for scoring and a heavier one for hewing; a crosscut or framesaw, or a power saw with a 16 or 18-inch bar; and an auger bit 2 inches wide. In addition, you will need a peeling spud (see Fig. 2); a couple of log dogs; a scriber; and a basic set of carpenter's tools. You might have a hard time finding some of these tools. Some you might have to have made by a blacksmith.

48

PEELING SPUD

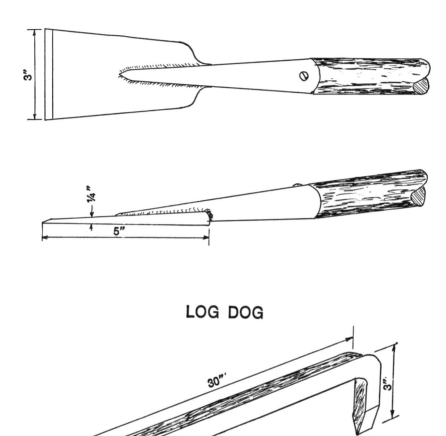

LOG DOG

Figure 2

*The peeling spud is used for removing bark from logs;
the log dog for anchoring logs when hewing.*

CROSS SECTION OF FOUNDATION

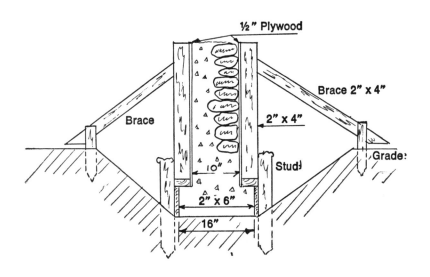

BROAD AXE

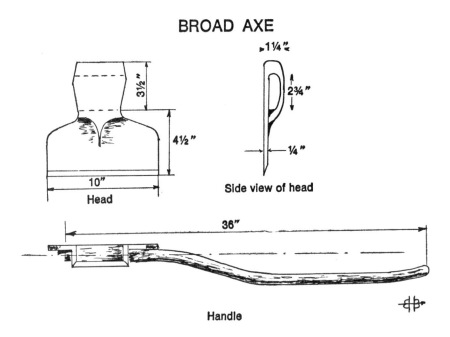

Head

Side view of head

Handle

THE FOUNDATION

Now we come to one of the most important parts of the whole building project — the foundation. The reason so many log buildings fall into disrepair is largely because they were built without proper foundations. This was often the case with pioneer buildings, since early settlers were often forced to build directly on the ground due to the limited amount of materials available to them. These log buildings often rested on small stones which one man could carry, and which the weight of the building soon drove into the ground. With a minimal amount of insulating air below the building the logs soon started to decay. Today we do not have this problem because we can provide a proper foundation and well-insulated floors. It is sometimes tempting to rush this part of the building project: you want to get going so as to have the building under roof before bad weather sets in. However, the importance of a good and proper foundation cannot be overlooked.

A good foundation need not be either complicated or expensive. I quite agree with B. Allan Mackie, the famous Canadian architect, that a basement is both a waste of money and time. Usually it provides a poor root cellar, expensive storage, and, with insufficient headroom, a hazard to life and limb. Frost will not affect a shallow foundation if it is properly drained — either drain tile or drain rock compacted around the footing is, in most cases, sufficient.

Before any digging can take place, you must lay out the foundation. To ensure that the foundation will be level and square, and to guide you for size, you have to set up batter boards (Fig. 3). First drive small stakes at each corner of the building, indicating the outside line of the foundation walls. If you do not have a surveyor's instrument to guide you to get the 90° angles necessary for square corners, use the triangle measuring method — measure along one side a distance in 3-foot units and along the adjacent end in 4-foot units. The diagonal will have an equal number of 5-foot units when the corner is square.

After locating the corners, drive three stakes at each corner at least 5 feet outside of the foundation line and nail horizontal boards to them. To ensure that these batter boards will be level, you can use a 50-foot ¾-inch water hose. Fasten one end of the water hose to the first corner post and run it along the side of the building line to the next corner post. Lift the hose well above the corner post and fill it with water. The water will seek its level and you will have a perfectly level line between corner 1 and corner 2. (See Fig. 3)

String or twine must be fastened to the batter boards and stretched taut to indicate the exact position of the outside of the foundation wall. Saw small notches in each of the batter boards so that if the lines are

LOCATING BUILDING WITH BATTER BOARDS

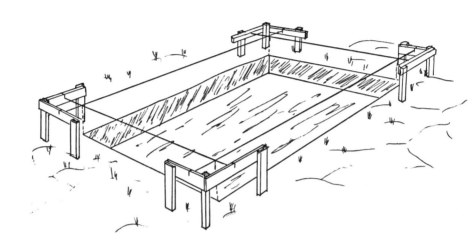

LEVELING BATTER BOARDS USING WATER HOSE

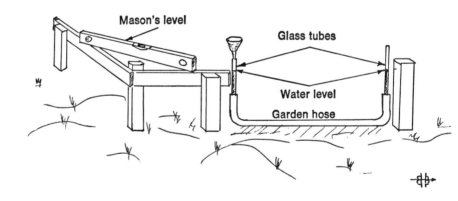

Figure 3

disturbed in any way they can be put back in exactly the same position as they were originally set up. Now check the diagonals — if they are equal, the building corners are square.

Now you are all set to start the backbreaking job of excavating the hole for your foundation, which should go at least one foot below the frost line. (Local building codes will tell you how deep the frost line is in your area.)

Before you start the actual foundation work, you must pour a footing. The footing should be at least 16 inches wide and at least 6 inches thick. The actual foundation wall should be 10 inches thick.

Low fieldstone or rock-wood foundations are most attractive for log buildings. Erect the back of the form for pouring the concrete against, and leave the front low. Place the rocks or the fieldstone towards the front and pour concrete behind them. Then you can add stone in the front as you go along and the finished work will look just as good as if an experienced mason had done the stonework.

If you have decided to include a fireplace in your building, now is the time to prepare a substantial foundation for it. I like to dig the foundation for the fireplace at least 4-feet deep, and it should protrude at least one foot wider all around than the fireplace is to be.

MIXING CONCRETE   The easiest way to mix the concrete is with a cement mixer. You can also do the mixing on a flat platform but it takes a lot of elbow grease. What proportions of gravel, sand, cement, and water should you use? Three parts of nut-sized aggregate (crushed stone), 2 parts sand, and 1½ parts cement, and just as much water as it takes to moisten the mixture. The amount of water is very important and you have to take into consideration the wetness of the sand and aggregate. If it has been raining the day before you need less water than if the material were sun dried.

With a log building it is wise to raise the end walls of the foundation half the thickness of the first logs going lengthwise. By doing this you save yourself the trouble of filling in the gap on the ends, and you get a better foundation. The foundation must be allowed to cure for at least 6 days. Concrete is considered to have obtained full strength after 28 days, but it is not necessary to wait that long since it will take at least this long before you have placed the full weight of the building on the foundation.

PREPARING THE LOGS

While you are waiting for the foundation to cure you should start preparing the logs for your building. Never peel or hew on your log

CHALKING

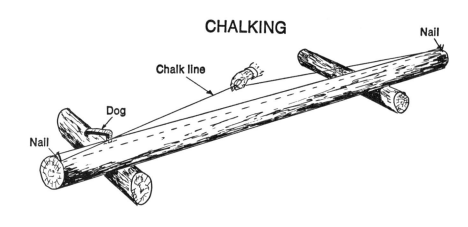

Nail

Chalk line

Dog

Nail

SCORING

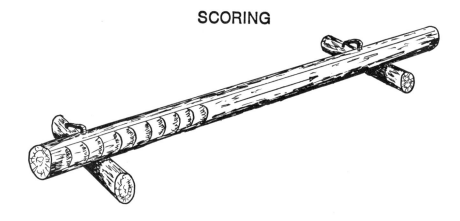

HEWING

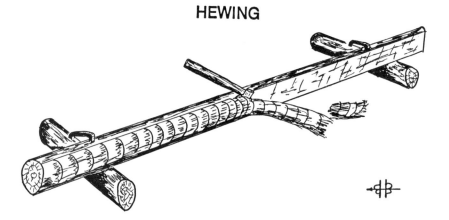

pile; it is unsafe because you may slip or the logs might move underfoot. In addition to the dangers, the peelings will clog your pile, making it impossible for you to see what you have or even to move the logs. A step ramp comes in handy now to take the logs down from the log pile. The step ramp is as old as building with logs. With the help of this invention even a single man can move a several-hundred-pound log from the ground to any height. When making the ramp, make sure you use strong enough logs because cutting out the steps in the log will weaken it considerably.

On a flat piece of ground immediately in front of the log pile, place two heavy logs on the ground crosswise to the pile. Then, with the help of the ramp, lift one log down on the logs and using the peeling spud, remove all the bark from the log. Never peel more logs than you can use within the next few days, because the bark on the logs is the best protection against mildew, checking, weathering, and other damage. Even after several years storage unpeeled logs look fresh. (Bark beetles will carve an intricate pattern on the logs, but to my way of thinking this only gives the logs a more interesting pattern.)

After the log has been peeled, use the log dogs. Drive the dogs with one end into the log you will be working on and the other end into the log that runs crosswise. In this manner the log will be securely fastened and will not roll when you start to score and hew. Snap a chalk line along the full length of the log by fastening one end of the line in the butt-end of the log with a nail, then drive a nail into the other end of the log. Stretch the line tightly and secure the loose end on the nail. Halfway between the nails, lift the line up and let it spring back towards the log and it will mark a straight line clearly on the log. Remove the line, and, with the smaller hewing axe stand on top of the log and vertically score cuts about 6 to 8 inches apart.

The score cuts should be deep enough to meet the chalk mark. The scoring is done to allow the slabs to break free without running in or out from the chalk mark. Now change to the heavier broad axe and start the actual hewing. Stepping back along the log as the work progresses, use strong strokes that are nearly straight down. These will slice off the slab along the chalk line on the log. This work is by far the hardest for the beginner as it requires a good deal of skill, a sure eye, and a lot of strength. Admiration for the old-time axe-men will increase with each stroke you take. Back home in Sweden I have seen a good axe-man peel and straight-hew 50 and more full-length logs in a day. As a matter of fact, I once saw four men put up a full-size lumber camp in two days.

LOG SCRIBER

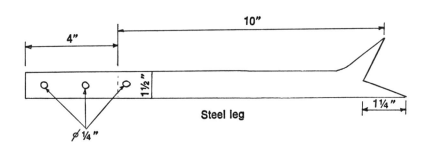

Steel leg

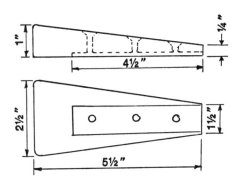

Wooden handle, side view (above) and looking down

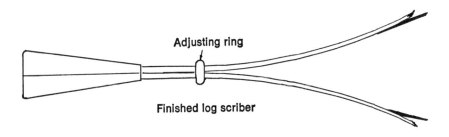

Adjusting ring

Finished log scriber

LOG CABIN CONSTRUCTION

THE FIRST STEPS   After you get 4 logs hewed, top and bottom, 2 long ones for the sides and 2 short ones for the ends, place the long logs on the foundation. These are to become the side walls, and run at right angles to the floor joists. It is important to remember to place the butt ends at the same end of the building. The next logs should be placed at right angles to the first ones, with the butts again the same way. Now begins the job of notching the corners of the logs soundly together. The round notch, with the timber sticking out about a foot in each corner, is the most practical and, to my way of thinking, the most attractive notch for a log building.

Place the end logs on top of the side logs, so that they overhang over the side logs by at least a foot and half. After the building is finished, cut all the corners to equal length. Now is the time to use the scribers to acquire the proper notch. Set the scribers to the widest space between the log and the foundation. Keep the cutting points vertical, that is, directly above one another, and hold the handle in as perfect a position as you can manage. Carry the scribed line up over the notch and onto the end of the log that extends past the wall. Scribe both the inside and the outside. Use the divider ends because the hooked points will not function here.

Turn the logs over and remove the wood within the scribed lines. Careful work now will create a notch that will require little or no chinking at all.

FLOOR JOISTS   The next step is cutting notches for the floor joists. The floor joists are medium-sized logs of about 8 to 10 inches in diameter and have to be hewn on one side to obtain a flat surface on which the sub-flooring eventually will rest. Floor joists should be placed on 16-inch centres to give you a solid floor. If the span of the building is more than 10 feet it will be necessary to place a support beam underneath. This support beam should run the whole length of the building and rest on stone cairns not farther apart than 10 feet. Wedges take up the space between the support log and the floor joists.

Using the chalk line, run a line halfway down on the side logs to mark the bottom of the seat for the floor joists.

The notches are made with the help of a handsaw and a 1-inch wood chisel. Cut the floor joist to proper length and square off the ends. It is important that all the square ends have the same measurement in height and width, measured from the flat surface; if not, the floor will be uneven. After all the joists are in I usually drill a 1-inch hole through

Round notch

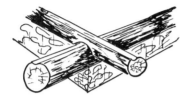

Dovetail

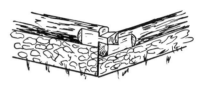

Scribed lines

Rough notch

Notch cut out

Scriber at work

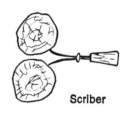

Scriber

the joist and the plate and drive a wooden peg in the hole. This will assure you that the plate log will not spread as the weight increases as the building goes up.

THE NEXT LAYER Next are the door openings. Mark them out on the plate log. You are now ready for the next layer of logs. Using the step ramp lift up the next long log, roll it over to the far side of the building, then choose a second long log for the near side. Place the log directly over the plate log, and scribe it all along its length, as well as the notch.

Turn the log over and secure it with the log dogs and start to hew the flat surface. After you get the flat surface hewn out and the notches cut, roll the log back in place and check to see if it fits the log below. Make necessary corrections to make the logs fit each other. Then roll the log back and cut a V-notch the full length of the log to accommodate the chinking or insulation in between the logs. The insulation can be moss gathered from the woods or strips of fiberglass matting.

Transfer the mark from the plate log to the second log and, with the 2-inch auger, drill a hole right through the second log about 4 inches back from the door opening. Mark on each side so that a mortise groove may be cut later in the log. Also at this time drill a hole in the sill log the same distance back from the door opening, but only halfway through the sill log. You have to repeat this operation with each log, going up around the door and window openings until the second round above the opening.

Fill the V-groove with fiberglass strips or moss and roll the log back into place and, presto, the job is done.

WALLS The appearance of your log building is largely dependent on how straight the walls are. You will see that they have a tendency to creep inwards as you go. Therefore it is important to have some means of keeping the walls straight and plumb.

A spirit level usually does not work well because of the unevenness of the logs. At this point you have to decide if you want the inside or the outside of the walls straight, or whether to line up the centre of the logs. Personally I like to line up the centre of the logs as this method gives a more natural look to the building. If you decide to line up the centre of the logs, use a plumb line. Before you cut each notch use the plumb line to make certain that each log is absolutely centred on top of the preceding log.

From here on it is a labor of love. As you go along you will gain more and more experience — the seams will get tighter, the notches more nearly perfect and your chest will begin to swell with pride.

PLATE AND FLOOR JOISTS

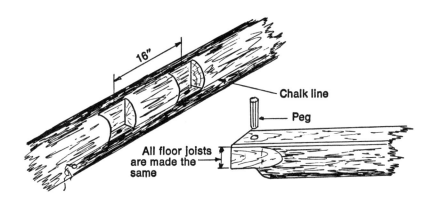

16"

Chalk line

Peg

All floor joists
are made the
same

DOOR AND WINDOW OPENINGS

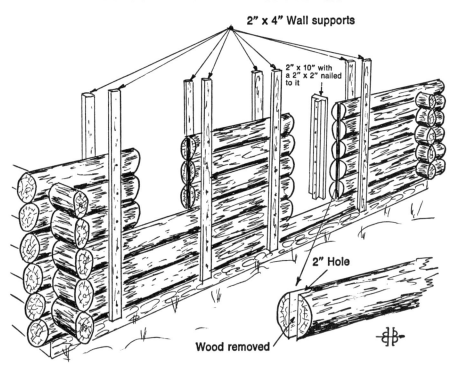

2" x 4" Wall supports

2" x 10" with
a 2" x 2" nailed
to it

2" Hole

Wood removed

The beauty of a log building that you yourself have built is that each log will harbor memories for the rest of your life. When sitting in your warm and cosy living room with a snowstorm raging outside, you may remember a particularly difficult-fitting log or maybe a scar on your hand or leg will remind you of a particular log, and you will feel justifiably proud.

CEILING BEAMS When the walls are the desired height it is time to consider gable ends and the slope of the roof. But before you start on this project place your ceiling beams in place. Square-hewn ceiling beams are much more attractive and more practical than round beams. The ceiling beams are notched in the same manner as the floor joists. They are also pegged to help hold the building together.

If you at this time put your ceiling beams in and cover them with planks it will give you a floor to work from and the erection of purlins, gable ends, and rafters becomes much simpler and the risk of an accident lessens. Do not nail the ceiling planks at this time, just make them secure enough so they will not move. Leave the planks to really dry before nailing them permanently to the ceiling beams.

GABLES The look of the building improves greatly if there are log gables. It may take more work but it pays off. First, decide on the pitch of the roof. The pitch of the roof is found by dividing the total height of the roof above the top plate (rise) by the total span of the building. Say, for instance, that the building spans 30 feet and the rise is 10 feet. The pitch is 10÷30 which equals ⅓ pitch. A roof with less pitch than 1/5 is not suitable for shake shingles and there will be undue stress on it under a snow load.

Now you must ascertain where the ridge pole is going to go. Drive a small nail partly into the outside of the top log at each corner and fasten wires to each. Measure 10 feet from the top log down on one end wall. Hammer in another nail and fasten the wires there. Loosen this middle nail and nail it to a long slender pole. Raise the pole up on top of the building until you have equal tension on both wires. This point will be the peak of the roof. Repeat this procedure at the other end of the building.

Place a log on the gable end — you might have to nail planks on the outside and the inside of the building to hold this log in place. Take the auger and drill a hole through the top log and the log directly beneath it. Drive a hardwood peg through the holes. Cut the ends of the logs along the wire you had strung to the peak. Work both ends at the same time. Having the ceiling planks in will save a lot of climbing up

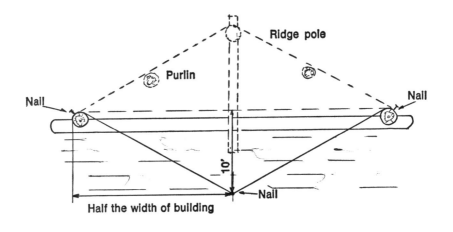

Ridge pole

Purlin

Nail

Nail

Nail

10'

Half the width of building

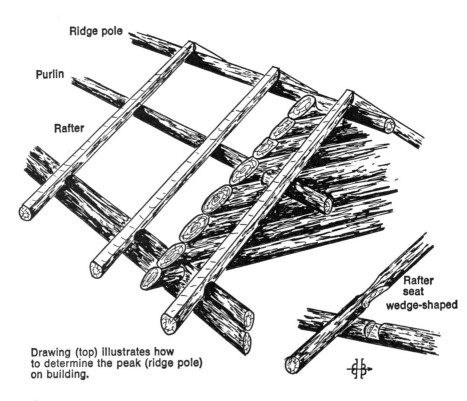

Ridge pole

Purlin

Rafter

Rafter
seat
wedge-shaped

Drawing (top) illustrates how
to determine the peak (ridge pole)
on building.

and down: you can walk on the top of the ceiling. One purlin is usually enough, halfway up to the peak beam.

RAFTERS   The next step is to fit the notched rafters into the side beams. The rafters should be cut to meet each other at the peak. The notch in the side beams for the rafter should be slightly narrowed at the outside and the rafter wedge-shaped, and driven into the notch. Leave the rafters a little longer at both ends. Lean the top ends from each side against the ridge pole and cut them together. After you have all the rafters up, measure the overhang, run a line along the whole length of the building, and cut them all the same length.

ROOFING   In the olden days it was not an unusual sight to see flowers growing on the roof of log buildings. The old-style turf roof served two purposes: during the growing season it was fireproof and it was a good insulator during the winter months. One disadvantage of a turf roof is its weight. Also you must have the proper long-grained grass with a heavy root system or the first rain will wash the earth away.

Cedar shakes or shingles are a far better roofing material. You do not have to sheet the roof completely but just run strapping on top of the rafters. As an extra precaution against a leaky roof, I put heavy rolled roofing under the shakes.

You can easily make your own shakes using a large cedar log which has started to decay in the middle. Cut the log into 20-inch-long pieces. Split these logs into four sections and leave them to dry. Have your blacksmith make you a "frobe" out of a car spring leaf. He will have to heat the whole spring, take out the slight curve, then re-harden it, and put an eye in one end. Put a wooden handle in the eye, make yourself a hardwood mallet, and you are ready to make your own shakes.

The shakes should be about ⅝ of an inch thick. When you cut them from the wooden block, turn the block end for end with each cut to assist taper. When you are ready to roof the building, start at the eaves and nail the shakes in the upper end to the strapping with 1½-inch galvanized nails. The next layer of shakes should come down a third of the length of the previous shake and should cover the split between the layer below. To help you obtain a straight line, run a chalk line along the roof.

INSULATION   Roof and floor insulation are most important if you are going to have a warm building. Before starting on the flooring, nail chicken wire to the floor joists, making pockets between the joists.

63

MAKING SHAKES

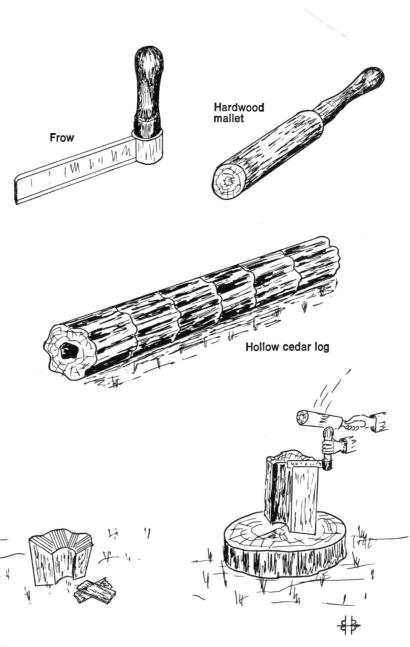

Frow

Hardwood mallet

Hollow cedar log

Place plastic sheeting on top of the chicken wire and fill the space or pockets with sawdust mixed with lime. (The lime will keep animals from making nests in the filling.) On the ceiling place a sheet of plastic, then place loose fiberglass insulation on top to a thickness of at least 6 inches.

FIREPLACE CONSTRUCTION

No log building is complete without a fieldstone fireplace. A raised hearth has the advantage of cutting down on floor drafts. An ash-removal door should be placed on the outside of the chimney. Always install a flue liner. A suitable mortar mix for masonry is: 1 part masonry cement, ¼ part Portland cement, and 3 parts wet mortar sand.

By using a prefabricated heat circulator unit, most of your worries will be over and you will be sure of a fireplace that will not smoke and will draw properly. Furthermore, the air circulated through the heatalator will add to the warmth of the room. The prefabricated heat circulator is a welded unit already equipped with draft control and damper, ready to build into the stonework.

If you decide to build your own fireplace here are a few rules that you should follow: Flue size should be calculated on the fireplace opening, and it should never be smaller than 8 by 12 inches. The front of the opening should be wider than the back, and the back should tilt forward to meet the throat. Make the vertical portion of the back about half the height of the opening. The back should not be less than two-thirds of the width of the opening.

Project the throat as far forward as possible to form a smoke shelf. Obtain a well-designed damper that fits the throat opening perfectly. Line the fireplace with fire brick and high-temperature cement. Make sure that the fireplace walls are thick enough for fire protection. Solid masonry walls should be not less than 8 inches thick and hollow masonry should be at least 12 inches thick.

Place the entire fireplace within the walls of the building, if at all possible. A hot chimney will draw much better and will store enough heat to keep the building warm all night long.

It is most important in a log building that the fireplace not be tied into the logs at all. As the logs shrink, you will get cracks between the logs which might even damage the fireplace. Leave 2 to 3 inches between the roof material and the logs. Leave 2 to 3 inches between the roof material and the chimney and use metal flashing around the stonework. Get a skilled chimney builder to construct your chimney.

FIREPLACE

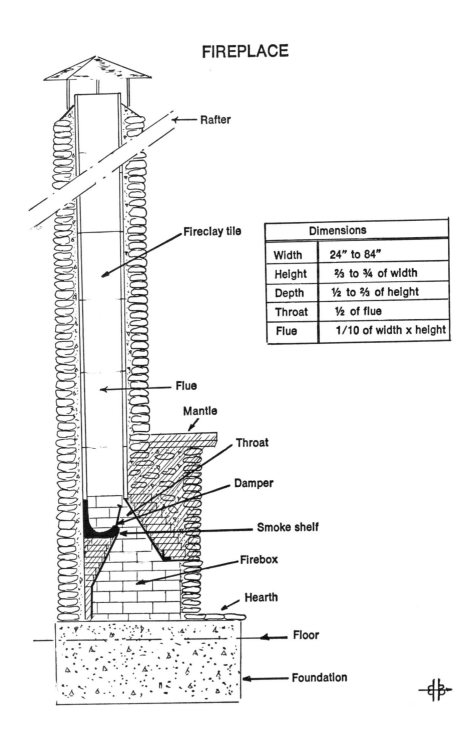

Dimensions	
Width	24" to 84"
Height	⅔ to ¾ of width
Depth	½ to ⅔ of height
Throat	½ of flue
Flue	1/10 of width x height

Rafter

Fireclay tile

Flue

Mantle

Throat

Damper

Smoke shelf

Firebox

Hearth

Floor

Foundation

THE FINISHING TOUCHES

Put in window and door frames, hang the windows and the doors and remember to chink with insulation material. The last step is to fit the facers (trim) inside and out. I leave it to your imagination and taste to put up partitions and interior decorations. Remember, if you are using logs for partitions, they have to be notched into the walls in such a manner that they will not bind the outside walls. Dovetailing is usually the best way to fasten the intersecting walls to the outside walls.

Good luck with your new log-building.

SAUNA

Usually the first building that settlers in the Scandinavian countries erected was the steambath or the sauna. This building, made of cedar logs, was about 12 by 15 square feet and served the settler and his family as temporary quarters while he broke ground and felled trees for the main building.

Cedar logs were usually used because of their pleasant aroma when wet and for their resistance to rot. The inside roof height was no more than 7 feet. This, of course, was to keep the heat down when the building was used as a sauna. It usually contained only one room, to be divided later by a partition for a wash and shower room. It is important that you never allow soap or any kind of shampoo in the actual steam room as they make the floor extremely slippery and in a short time the fat from the soap in the extreme dry heat will give off a foul smell.

We built our sauna by pouring a slab of concrete 6 inches thick directly on undisturbed ground and erected the cedar log building on top of this. The fireplace is of a slightly different construction from the chimney and the fire doors are placed outside the building. The only part of the fireplace that is inside is the square box that holds the small round stones. The steam in a sauna is created by throwing cold water on the heated stones.

I used a 45-gallon drum as a firebox. The drum is placed horizontally in the lower part of the chimney with the closed end towards the steam room. Around this drum I built the chimney and the square box to hold the stones. The stones should rest on the bare metal inside the box to facilitate heat transfer from the firebox to the stones. A good damper was purchased and placed in the throat of the chimney, to control the draft. In the final stages of the firing it is closed off almost entirely to keep the heat on the stones.

SAUNA

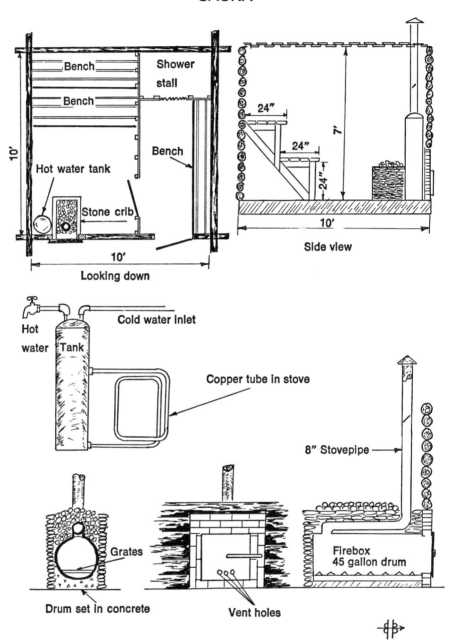

Bench

Shower stall

Bench

Bench

10'

Hot water tank

Stone crib

10'

Looking down

24"

7'

24"

24"

10'

Side view

Cold water inlet

Hot water Tank

Copper tube in stove

8" Stovepipe

Grates

Drum set in concrete

Vent holes

Firebox
45 gallon drum

68

Inside the steam room I erected two tiers of seats. The more hardy use the upper tier for more heat while the less hardy enjoy the lesser heat on the lower tier.

I also equipped the washroom with a shower, because it is important after a steambath to have an ice-cold shower to close the pores of the skin. In winter, with snow on the ground, you can of course get out and roll in the snow.

The hot-water system was installed by running a copper pipe outside, fastened to the 45-gallon drum with electric cable clips, connected to the water system at one end and to an old, discarded water-heater tank at the other end. While the steambath is heating, the water in the hot-water tank heats to boiling and is ready for use.

SMOKEHOUSE

Curing fish and meat by smoking has been carried out for many centuries. It is known that both early man and the Indians used wood smoke to cure and preserve fish and meat. The process of smoke curing involves not only the actual smoking, but also salting, drying, and heat-treating the meat and fish. The final results depend largely on the skill and experience of the operator, quality of control, and, of course, on the quality of the meat and fish. But just as important is the actual smoking equipment.

There are three types of simple smokehouses: the converted icebox or refrigerator, the oil drum screen and washtub, the wooden-barrel type. All three will do the job, but the Cadillac of them all is the permanent smokehouse. Here is what you do.

Build a foundation of cement blocks 4 feet square and 2 feet high. Dig a ditch about 18 inches deep and 10 feet long, to accommodate the smoke pipe. At the end of the ditch, make the firebox. The firebox should be about 3 feet in diameter and 2 feet deep with the bottom and the sides lined with firebricks.

Leave an opening in the firebox for the smoke pipe, which can be an ordinary 6-inch stovepipe starting in the box and ending in the middle of the foundation. Put an elbow on the short pipe coming out of the foundation, and add a common stovepipe damper with an extended handle to reach outside the foundation, so that you can regulate the heat and the smoke from there. Cover the pipe with earth or sand.

The pipe coming out of the foundation has to have a smoke spreader. This can be a galvanized water pail with a number of ¾-inch holes punched in the sides and bottom. Place the pail directly over the mouth of the pipe and it will distribute the smoke evenly throughout the house.

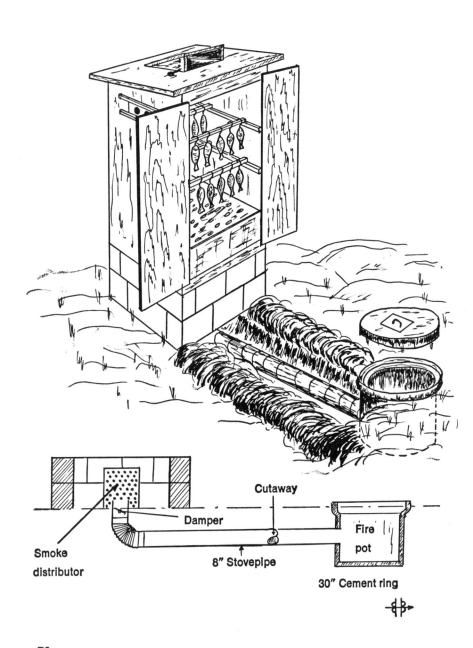

Cutaway

Damper

Smoke
distributor

8" Stovepipe

Fire
pot

30" Cement ring

Now you are ready for the superstructure — a small wooden building 4 feet square and 7 feet high with a sloping roof. The whole front consists of 2 doors.

Install a trip ventilator in the roof to let the smoke escape. Or a series of 2-inch holes can be drilled just underneath the roof, and sliding covers be made to go over them to regulate the amount of smoke you want to escape.

About 12 inches from the bottom of the house, install a false floor and drill a series of holes with a 1-inch bit at 2-inch intervals. On the two sides, wooden battens should be nailed at 12-inch intervals to support the sticks on which the fish will be hung, or to support the screen trays for meat or cheese.

Nail a double thickness of burlap just below the roof to absorb the moisture that will form on wet or rainy days on the ceiling of the smokehouse.

A square piece of metal with a draft-control hole over the fire pit completes the installation. Now you are ready to try out the first of your own smoked meat or fish.

CHAPTER 5

Twenty-Two Horses
Come to the Homestead

TRACTORS

Soon after you start homesteading, you will realize how necessary it is
to have a helper. This helper can be a horse or, as in our case, a small
tractor.

After talking to several farmers in our area it seemed that a tractor
in the 25 to 30-horsepower range would be ideal for our use. This tractor is not always big enough but it is relatively inexpensive and can do
about 90 per cent of all the necessary work in the first few years.

If you live in a farming community there are two ways to go about
acquiring a used tractor. First, drop the word that you are looking for
a small tractor and you will find there are many sitting around on farms
not in use. The second way is to watch for farm auctions. The farm auction is usually a community affair, with equipment, tools, and furnish-
ings from several farms in the area offered for sale. Often old, smaller
pieces of equipment will be sold at very reasonable prices.

This was how we acquired our small 22-horsepower Ford tractor. It
is big enough to pull stumps and stones as well as the two-furrow plough
and the smaller disc. It is maneuverable enough to get around the trees
in our bush when we are hauling out logs or using wagon or sleigh to
gather maple sap.

Our tractor is equipped with a three-point hook-up system and a
power take off. The PTO furnishes power to a grass cutter, post-hole
digger, and gives me enough power to drive a 28-inch circular saw blade.
I have a belt-pulley assembly that can be used in three alternate positions: by using different pulley sizes I can get the speed I require on the
driven axle. With the help of the alternate positions of the drive pulley,
I can get the desired directions of the belt.

73

Pulling forces (on a tractor, a drive wheel equipped with rubber tires) are concentrated at a point near ground level and directly below the centre of the rear axle. It is important to have the hitch point as low as possible to increase the front wheel weight on the tractor. This ensures a safe level for steering purposes as well as enough weight on the front so the tractor will not flip over backwards when under heavy load. Often people not familiar with this will hook up a load from the top link or the rear axle. This is a very dangerous practice.

In most farming operations it is desirable to increase the weight of the wheels to get better traction. As water freezes, the tires are filled with a calcium chloride solution which has the advantage of a low freezing point and a higher weight per gallon than water. In some cases, even the front wheels are filled with this solution to add more front-end weight to the tractor. However, with an intelligent draw-bar hook-up, this is not necessary. Fluid in the tires has the advantage of placing weight where it is needed and not interfering with tractor use. Weight added to a tractor results in a higher consumption of fuel and an added load on the engine; therefore weight should be added only if necessary.

Four-Wheel Construction

Field crops determine row clearance and wheel spacing. (On most tractors the wheels can be turned inside out to provide different row spacing). Additional tractor stability is obtained from having the tractor weight as low as possible and the use of four-wheel construction. A low four-wheel tractor can be turned quickly and safely. What is a safe turning speed on level ground may not be safe on a slope. A negative bank of 20 degrees will reduce the safe turning speed about 25 per cent.

Hitch Construction

Drawbar linkage is designed as a built-in safety feature. If the front end should start to rise under load, the drawbar can be lowered rapidly to greatly reduce the effectiveness of the force tending to overturn the tractor.

Safe Starting

It is necessary for the transmission to be shifted to neutral before the starting motor can be operated through the starter button. This prevents starting the engine when the tractor is in gear and greatly reduces the possibility of a serious accident.

Power Take Off Shield

The shield on the power take off adapter meets the standards of the American Society of Agricultural Engineers. Always use the power take off shield. It is provided for your protection.

DANGEROUS CONDITIONS

The following dangerous conditions should be carefully noted. By following the simple precautions given here, accidents can be avoided.

Rear Wheels Frozen to the Ground If the rear tractor wheels are frozen to the ground, it is possible for the tractor to rotate around the rear axle. Under these conditions it is advisable to back the tractor to free the wheels. The front wheels of the tractor will not rise in reverse gear. If backing the tractor is impossible, be prepared to disengage the clutch quickly while attempting to move forward.

Very High Hitch The tractor hitch is the part of the tractor designed for pulling. Pulling from the top link, or from the axle housing can cause the front end of the tractor to rise under ordinary loads. *Always hitch to the drawbar.*

AVOIDING ACCIDENTS

Follow these rules to avoid accidents:
1. Reduce the speed on turns.
2. If the front end tends to rise, use reverse gear. If the tractor must move forward, be prepared to disengage the clutch.
3. When pulling, use the drawbar.
4. Use good judgment when pulling loaded wagons in high gear.

Your tractor has many built-in safety features; good judgment, however, is the best accident preventative.

TRACTOR TOOLS

Stone Hooks

This simple implement is invaluable for picking up stones from fields. The hooks are mounted on the three-point hook-up system and are dropped by the hydraulic system to engage the tines of the hook below the stones. As the tractor moves forward, the hooks will sink in under the stone and lift the stone out of the ground. *Warning.* Keep an eye on the front end of the tractor so it will not rise off the ground. The stone you have hooked might be bigger than you estimated. Never take

STONE HOOKS

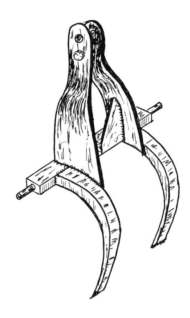

STONE BOAT

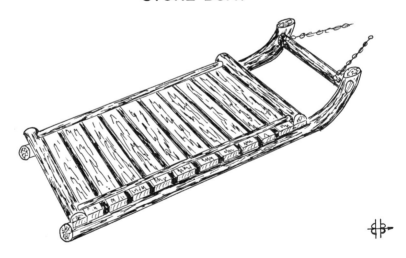

Steel hooks, such as the one shown above, are useful for lifting stones.
A stone boat eases the burden of transporting stones.

76

a run at a stone you intend to remove. A sudden stop on the run might cause the tractor to flip over.

Plows

There are many different plows on the market, but the most important thing to remember when you are looking for one is to get one suitable for your tractor. Any dealer in used farm equipment can tell you which is the right plow for your purpose. If you attend a farm auction and are not familiar with the different plows and their uses, ask a farmer to tell you if he thinks the plow for sale would suit your tractor.

I cannot tell you how to plow because it depends on so many factors: soil conditions, depth of furrows, what crop is to be grown on the land, to name a few. The best advice I can give is to talk to a local farmer and maybe hire him for a couple of days to show you how it is done.

Harrows

This tillage instrument smooths and pulverizes the soil and leaves the land in excellent condition for receiving the seed. Originally a harrow was a tree limb with short stubs of branches for teeth. Then it developed into a log with wooden pins set into it at intervals for teeth. Finally came the *spring-tooth harrows* that we use today — a series of springs attached to metal frames in several rows. The springs are adjustable to go deep or shallow, depending on the soil. The spring harrow is an ideal implement to use on stony ground.

DISC HARROW This implement does the same work as the spring harrow except it is not as good on stony ground. The disc will jump out of the ground when it hits a stone and will leave part of the ground uncultivated.

Blade

The blade is hooked up in the three-point hook-up system and is mainly used to clear ground in the same way as the bulldozer blade: it digs in, clears, and levels. It is good to use to back-fill around foundations, to level and spread gravel on the driveway, and to remove snow.

Stone Boat

This implement comes in handy for removing large stones or for hauling stones for building foundations. It is made from two naturally curved logs used for runners on which 2 x 6-inch planks are nailed crosswise to form a platform. Because this implement is so low to the ground, stones can be rolled up easily onto the platform, and, with a chain attached to the front of the logs, can be hauled away with the tractor. If you want to use it a great deal, have a blacksmith line the runners with steel shoes, made of ¼ x 3-inch steel bands.

Farm Wagons

A wagon will come in handy for many chores. It can be made out of an old car rear end for rear wheels, but remember, the front wheels have to turn to follow the tractor. An adjustable tongue connecting the front wheels and the rear wheels is a must, as this will allow you to adjust the length of the wagon.

Different kinds of boxes are made for different purposes — one for hauling manure, another with a solid bottom with a lighter outrigger for hauling hay and grain, and so on.

CHAPTER 6

Snow Drifts and Chores

In the middle of December we awoke one morning to find that the first snowstorm had blanketed our farm in six-foot drifts. "How lovely and clean everything looks!" my wife exclaimed, leaning well out the window for a better view. "How deep are the snow drifts?" my daughter yelled coming through the bedroom door. "Dad do you think the school bus can make it?" It was obvious that it would take several hours to shovel a path to the barn, get the tractor started, and clear the lane down to the concession road.

The tractor and blade had been ready for over a month and I had been secretly hoping for a light snowfall to let me get acquainted with the techniques of snow removal. I could remember my father's voice explaining the importance of clearing a road twice its width the first time, because after each snowfall and subsequent clearing the road gets narrower and narrower. But this was secondary at the moment; first things first, and that meant grabbing the old-fashioned snow shovel.

After dressing lightly, my first task was to slowly open the door and recover the snowshovel that I thought I had placed outside the door. It wasn't there. Then I remembered that during the frequent October rains I had used it to make small ditches in the sand to drain the water away from our front door. Now I had to wade through waist deep snow to find it, with my wife's voice reminding me that this was my usual way of doing things; spending numerous hours looking for tools and implements that I never remembered to put back in their proper place. Telling myself that this would be the last time any tools would be left lying around, I promptly broke that promise, although it was the next snowstorm before I realized that the shovel and the snowshoes had been left in the barn. But, believe me, after that experience, I would rather take the constant kidding of my friends about the shovel and snowshoes sitting close to the front door from early fall right through to spring.

After this early December snowfall, all outdoor work ceased and it was time to start the numerous winter projects I had lined up. We had ordered bees for spring delivery, so the most important task was to provide proper housing for the 27,000 honey-makers when they arrived in April.

BEEHIVES

After studying several books about bees and beekeeping we decided to build the standard hive used in North America, named after the inventor, L. L. Langstroth, who discovered the "bee space" principle in 1851. This space, one quarter of an inch to three eighths of an inch, is an area around frames just wide enough to allow a bee to pass through. Bees will not fill this space with propolis or burr comb. A beehive made to the inventor's specifications is called The Standard Langstroth Hive.

Any person handy with tools can construct his own beehives and frames quite readily. But one word of warning: make sure you adhere rigidly to the standard measurements given in the building instructions, otherwise you will run into trouble later when obtaining the foundation wax from a bee-supply house. It is designed to fit the standard frames and when the time comes to place the frames in the supers they must fit. This is not only important for the exterior measurements, but also for the measurement of frames and spacing tabs on the frames. The spacing tabs are vitally important. If they are too narrow, the frames will sit too close in the boxes and may create a problem in swarm control. If the space tabs are too wide, the frames are too far apart and the bees build burr combs, which fasten the frames and other moveable parts of the hive together, and make them very difficult to operate.

A standard hive unit for normal production consists of one bottom board, three to five boxes which can be used for either brood chambers or honey supers, one inner top cover, and an outer top cover which should be metal-covered. In addition you will need queen excluders and hive stands. (Fig. 1)

Materials

White pine is by far the best material for both the hive body and the other components of the hive; basswood may be used for the frames. After the hive has been assembled the exterior should be painted a pale blue.

ASSEMBLING A BEEHIVE

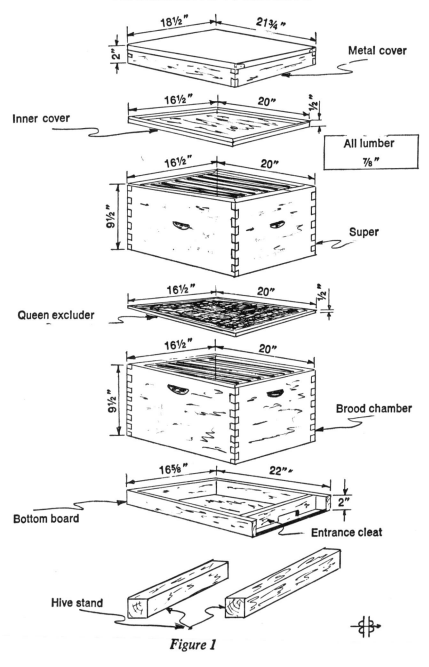

Figure 1

HIVE FRAME DETAIL

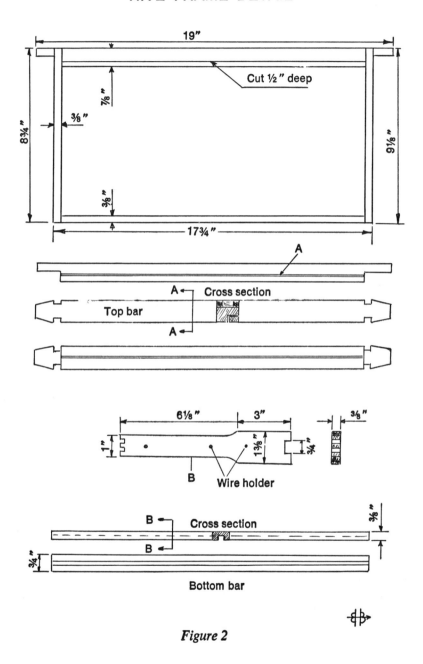

Figure 2

FRAMES Building this part of the hive is the most time-consuming operation, and you have to be patient and accurate. If you are not, trouble will lie in wait for you when you begin installing the foundation wax in the frames.

TOP BAR The top bar is made from a board ⅞ of an inch thick, cut into 1-inch strips each 19 inches long. Each strip must have a groove half an inch wide and ¼-inch thick (see A in Fig. 2). This can be cut with the saw and will eventually hold the foundation wax in place.

SIDES The sides are made out of blocks of wood 1½ inches thick and, after the spacer notches are cut, the blocks are then cut into strips ¼-inch thick. (see B in Fig. 2)

BOTTOM Bar A board ¾-inch thick and 17¾ inches long is cut into ¼-inch strips, and in the middle of each strip the saw is run to create a cut about halfway through. (C in Fig. 2)

Cuts and notches are then made to assemble the frame. The frames are nailed together with special nails obtained from a bee-supply house.

After the frames have been assembled, four holes, ⅛ of an inch in diameter, must be drilled in the sides of the frames to accommodate the foundation wire. (D in Fig. 2)

To make the job faster and more accurate, make a nailing box which will enable you to assemble 10 frames at a time.

In order to install the foundation wax you need a board to hold the frames square. The wax is placed in the frames and welded with an imbedding tool. This tool must be dipped in hot water to partially melt the wax so that the wires can be imbedded in the wax.

You will need 10 frames for the brooder body and 9 frames for each super. It is wise to make at least three supers to each brooder body so the bees will have enough room to store their honey. If there is not enough room for them during the honey season, the risk of swarming will increase considerably.

SUGARING SPOUTS

After the beehives, my next project was also geared for early spring use. We have about 2,000 sugar maples on our property and we planned to tap the trees in the spring.

When the Indians tapped maple trees they simply made a V-shaped cut in the bark of the tree and inserted a piece of birchbark in the cut to act as a drip board, and then placed a hollowed-out log underneath to collect the sap.

WOOD SPOUT

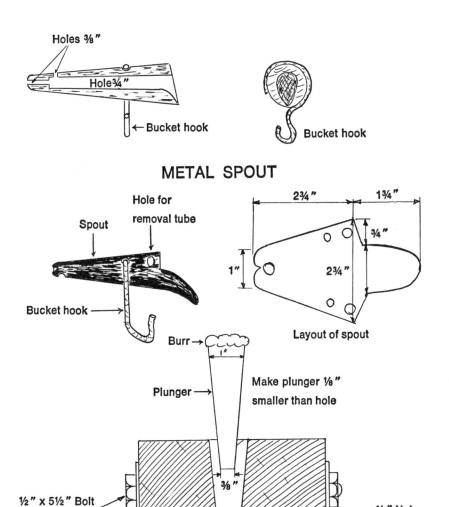

Holes ⅜"

Hole ¾"

← Bucket hook

Bucket hook

METAL SPOUT

Spout

Hole for removal tube

Bucket hook →

2¾"   1¾"

¾"

1"   2¾"

Layout of spout

Burr →

1"

Plunger →

Make plunger ⅛" smaller than hole

⅜"

½" x 5½" Bolt →

½" Nut

½" Washer

Hardwood die

Figure 3

Making wood and metal spouts for collecting maple syrup.

PACKBOARD

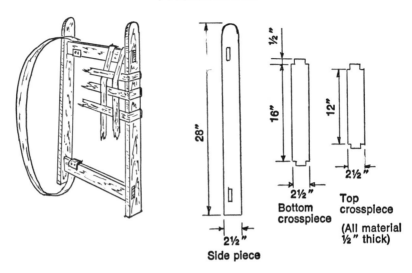

28"

2½"
Side piece

½"

16"

2½"
Bottom
crosspiece

12"

2½"
Top
crosspiece

(All material
½" thick)

CORN OR BEAN PLANTER

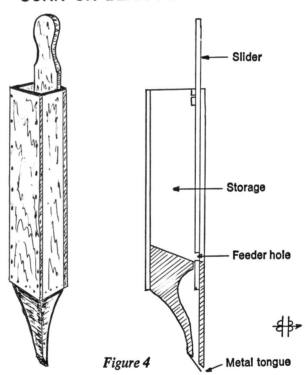

Slider

Storage

Feeder hole

Metal tongue

Figure 4

When the white man first learned the value of maple sap, he improved the tapping method by drilling a hole in the tree trunk to insert a spout made of wood; later a piece of metal formed as a tap was (and still is) used.

The very latest tapping method is to use nylon tubing leading from the spouts on each tree to a gathering tank. This eliminates the strenuous labor of walking from tree to tree, emptying each bucket into a larger container. Spouts can be obtained from a maple-syrup supply house but I decided to make my own wood and metal spouts.

Wood Spouts   The wood used should be a hardwood; oak or white ash is ideal. If you have a wood lathe it is easy to make wood spouts, if not the hardwood dowels can be whittled into shape with a knife. (Fig. 3). After the shape has been obtained, a hole must be drilled or burned lengthwise in the spout. The diameter of the hole should be at least ¾ inches and must not go all the way through. A small hole, ⅜ of an inch, is then drilled in the small end at a 90° angle from the other hole, and should be placed on the underside of the spout. (Fig. 3)

Wood spouts can only be used for one or two seasons, after which they will be so badly worn that they have to be replaced.

Metal Spouts   To make metal spouts I use 16-gauge galvanized steel that can be purchased from a hardware store at a reasonable price. The steel is cut with metal snips to conform with the illustration shown here. If you plan to make many spouts, make a die out of hardwood. (Fig. 3)

After you have roughly rolled the metal, place it in the hole of the die and insert the plunger. Give it a hard tap with the hammer and you have a perfectly formed spout. All you have to do now is to fold the tab over and drill the holes for the bucket hook and the opening hole in the small end of the spout. Here again drill the hole ⅜ of an inch in diameter and place it on the underside of the spout.

PACKBOARDS

A homemade packboard is almost a must for the settler. It can be used for carrying home shopping from the store or a quartered moose after the kill. I have seen many different models of packboards but will describe the one I think is the best.

White ash is the best wood for the frame because it is strong and light. If ash is not available, oak may be used, but it will make the packboard slightly heavier.

Cut two strips 2½ inches wide, half an inch thick, and about 28 inches long, to use for the sides of the frame. Round the top ends, but leave the bottom ends square. Now cut two pieces 2½ inches wide and ¾ of an inch thick, one piece 12 inches long and the other 16 inches. Join these cross pieces to the sides by cutting slots in the sides (mortise) and form a tongue on the cross pieces (tenon) making them fit well. Glue the joints together. (Fig. 4) The top of the upper cross piece should sit 3 inches above the bottom ends of the side pieces.

Lace nylon webbing, the kind that you can obtain for re-webbing garden chairs, over the frames. I have seen packboards with a solid canvas cover but I have found them to be hot on the trail. Fold the ends of the webbing double and insert two grommets in each end. Lace on the back side of the frame (the straps should be at least two inches short to allow you to pull the webbing very tight). (Fig. 4)

Now attach the shoulder straps at the upper end closely together in the centre of the upper crossbar and secure to the outside of the side pieces of the frame with one, 1-inch buckle on each side. I have found that the best straps are made out of heavy chrome-tanned leather saturated with silicone boot preservative. The shoulder straps should be 2 inches wide at the top where they go over the shoulders and taper off to 1 inch for under the armpits. If they are too wide at this point chafing of the armpits will occur. A canoe pack or just a square piece of canvas can be laced onto this packboard to contain whatever you want to carry.

CORN OR BEAN PLANTERS

Seeding corn, peas, or beans is a back-breaking job, but it can be made as easy as a walk in the fields with a walking stick. The walking stick is replaced by the planter. The construction is simple, as many of our early tools were often made on the homestead with crude tools and a limited selection of wood.

Out of a clear pine board cut two strips 4 inches wide, ½ inch thick, and about 36 inches long. These pieces will form the container for the seed. The tip of the planter is made from a solid piece of hardwood, and the container is fastened to the tip with glue and small nails. Inside, the container is a long strip of wood held in place by smaller strips and allowed to slide up and down. A small adjustable hole in the bottom will feed the tip with one seed at a time. A piece of metal is fastened on the tip to cover the opening when the planter is pushed down in the earth but will open when the planter is withdrawn, depositing one seed at a time. (Fig. 4)

LOG CABIN FURNITURE

BEDS Double-decker sleeping accommodation is commendable in many ways. It is a space saver and is also warmer in cold weather. Anyone who has spent many nights in the top section of one of these beds is not likely to make the mistake of adding frills to the bed, which makes it more picturesque but interferes with air circulation. A comfortable bed is a must for the settler. One of the best beds is the spring-pole bunk bed. Do not fix the bed to the wall; it is impractical when you have to move the furniture. Here is how to make it.

The need for storage space in your wilderness home usually governs the height of the bed but should not be less than 30 inches. The area beneath may accommodate drawers or shelves. You may find it more convenient to close in the space with doors or sliding panels and use it to store boxes or duffle bags.

You will need four lengths of small tree trunks 5 inches in diameter and about 6 feet long for the corner posts; four tree trunks about 5 inches in diameter and 7 feet 6 inches long for the sides; four pieces, 6 inches in diameter and 3 feet long to make up the ends. Twenty saplings, about 1-inch thick, will make up the springs.

Remove the bark, either with an old-style draw-knife, or with a small long-handled metal floor scraper, and lay out the four corner posts on the floor, marking the outlines for the slots (or mortises) on all four posts at the same time. This will ensure that all slots are the same height. Each post will require four holes. (Fig. 5) I use a 1½-inch drill to drill several holes close together through the posts, then a wood chisel easily cleans out the wood between them to make a straight, smooth hole.

Now make tenons or tongues on the side pieces to fit into the slots. Placing the holes or slots at different heights on the posts and using wedges to lock them in, gives the bed the opportunity of being tightened as it loosens in the joints by driving the wedges in a bit more.

In the four end pieces, drill a series of 1-inch holes 1 inch apart to accommodate the small saplings that will be the springs. (Fig. 5)

After the bed has been assembled, the saplings must be threaded through the holes. With a saw, make a small cut in the large end of the sapling to take a small wedge which will hold the sapling in place. Only one end should be threaded this way, as the opposite end must move freely through the hole to give a spring effect.

A piece of styrofoam 6 inches thick and cut to size completes the bed. Instead of styrofoam you could make a mattress cover and fill it with recently cut, sun-dried hay or fluff from cattails. If you use the

SPRING-POLE BUNK BED

Figure 5

SPLIT LOG SETTEE

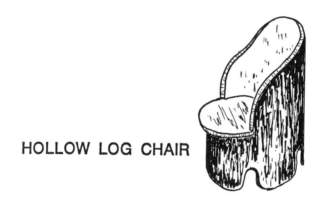

HOLLOW LOG CHAIR

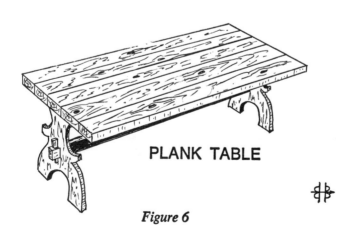

PLANK TABLE

Figure 6

BUTTER BOWL

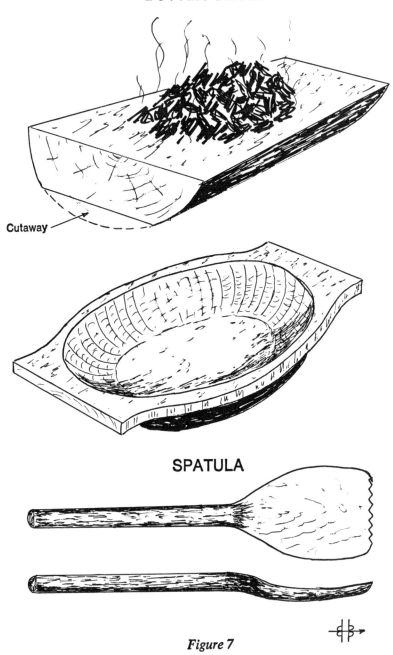

Cutaway

SPATULA

Figure 7

latter, make sure the fluff is dry; then sprinkle it with crushed mothballs. This will keep out small insects and worms that often are harbored in the fluff, and will give the mattress a fresh, fragrant smell.

CHAIRS, SETTEES AND TABLES   All can be made of split logs. They are not only necessary but also add a rustic touch to the interior of a cabin. For a table, look for a log 24 or more inches long, then split it in half, smooth the cut surface with a woodplane and then sand with sandpaper. Bore four 1½-inch holes on an angle from the bottom to accommodate the legs, taking care that you do not bore through the log.

Fit the legs. Make a small saw cut in the end that is going into the log. Make a wedge to fit, making sure that the wedge protrudes about half an inch over the end of the leg. Place the fitted leg into the hole and drive it home. The wedge protruding on top of the leg will hit the bottom of the hole, split the leg, and wedge it into the hole. (Fig. 6)

Turn your piece over and measure all legs to the same length. This is done easily by placing it on a flat surface, marking off the length you want with a 1-inch board measure. Move the board to the next leg and mark it. Proceed in this manner until all the legs are marked, then cut them off with a saw. They should all be the same length.

For a chair or settee, drill holes for the back and use the same method as with the legs to fasten the uprights to the seat with wedges. The top bar should be attached the same way.

When you see how beautiful the furniture is, you will want to make more and more, but remember it is easy to overcrowd a cabin. Thoreau rightly said that three chairs in a wilderness cabin were enough: "One for solitude, two for friendship, three for society."

BUTTER BOWL

To live off the land it is necessary to have some simple implements for making butter and cheese.

To work the buttermilk out of butter, a butter bowl and two spatulas are required. The butter bowl is best made out of a split log from a 12-inch basswood trunk. Smooth the split sides of the tree trunk with a woodplane, then take a hollow wood chisel and groove the surface in the middle of the log. Place a few live coals from the fire on top of the log. The coals will soon burn out the bulk of the wood in the log, but watch that they do not burn right through. When the desired depth has been burned, rake out the coals and, with the wood chisel, clean out

JUICE OR CHEESE PRESS

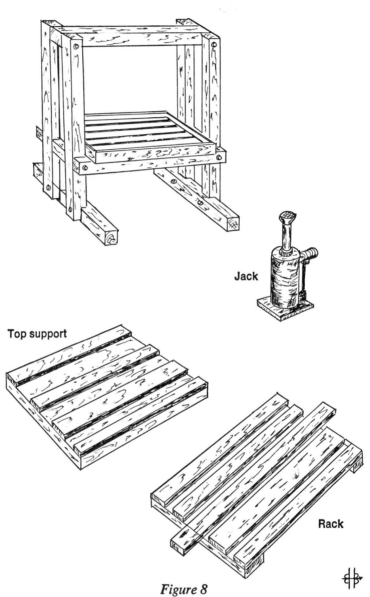

Jack

Top support

Rack

Figure 8
Whey is wrapped in cheesecloth, put on cheese mold; rack is inserted on
top. Finally the top support is put in — the jack then presses it all down.

all the charcoal. (Fig. 7) To finish the bowl, sand inside and out. You now have an attractive wooden bowl that will come in very handy.

Wood spatulas for kneading butter are also best made out of birch or basswood. (Fig. 7)

CHEESE PRESS

Cheese-making is simple and lots of fun, and, if you are a long way from a store, it is a necessity. Also, during the summer it is a good way to dispose of excess milk from your cows or goats.

To be able to make cheese you need a cheese press, and here is a simple but effective press which, with a spare set of top and bottom boards, will double as a fruit press for juices and cider. Get a few pieces of 4 x 4 inch pine, some lengths of threaded rods, nuts, and washers, an old car jack or a ¾-ton hydraulic jack and you are all set to go.

Assemble the frame, following the instructions in Fig. 8. The bottom board should be made out of 2-inch hardwood 14 x 14 inches. This size is not necessary for cheese-making but is good for a fruit press. The form or cast for the cheese can be a straight-sided milk pail with the bottom cut out. The plunger (to press the cheese) is made out of two layers of hardwood, separated by a ¾-inch sheet of plywood. (Fig. 8)

Underneath the bottom board you have to have a collector for the whey or fruit juice. In the middle of this collector pan, drill a 1-inch hole and insert in it a piece of 1-inch plastic hose long enough to reach under the pressing board.

In order to use the press for fruit, add five racks made out of ¼ x 1 inch and ¼ x 1½ inch hardwood, with the wider slats at the edges. The centre slat should be 8 inches longer and serve as a guide between the uprights. (Fig. 8) All nails that will come in contact with the juice or whey should be of stainless steel. For juice-making a form that is made out of ¾-inch hardwood, 2 inches wide and 14 x 14 inches long is needed.

BUTTER CHURN

Butter made on the homestead is not the ring-streaked, spotted material that you are used to from the store, but a product with the fragrance of green grass and the aroma of clover fields. It is simple and fun to make. You can make small quantities in a cleaned bottle by shaking the cream until it becomes butter, but more than likely you want larger quantities. With simple tools and materials you can produce a fairly good butter churn.

95

BUTTER CHURN

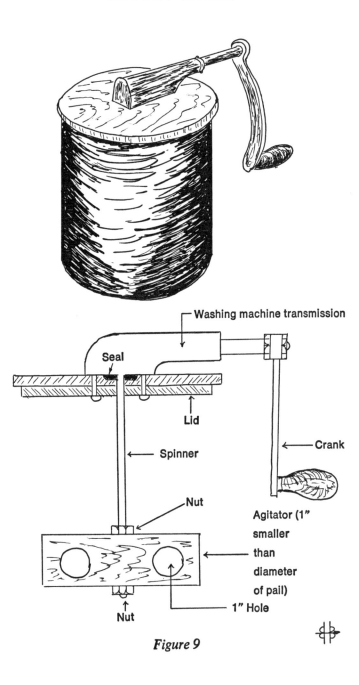

Washing machine transmission

Seal

Lid

Spinner

Crank

Nut

Agitator (1" smaller than diameter of pail)

Nut

1" Hole

Figure 9

Materials required are: a plastic straight-sided container holding about 2 gallons, a discarded washing-machine transmission, two pieces of hardwood, a wooden lid, and a crank.

First make a lid of plywood or hardwood to fit the top of the plastic container. Make this a snug fit so that it will not leak when using the churn. Drill a hole in the centre of the lid just large enough to accommodate the shaft from the washing-machine transmission. (Fig. 9)

To avoid leaks around the shaft, countersink the hole in the lid and use old-fashioned lamp wick material as a seal. Have a machine shop thread the shaft from the transmission about 6 inches up from the bottom. Cut two pieces of hardwood ¾ x 3 inches wide which is 2 inches smaller than the diameter of the plastic pail. Drill two, 1-inch holes in each end of the larger piece and then drill a hole through the small pieces to accommodate the threaded shaft. (Fig. 9) Screw a nut on the shaft as far as the thread goes, then put on a washer. Push the first hardwood piece on the shaft and another washer and nut to secure the wooden block. (The large piece with the two holes.) Repeat the performance with the second block.

Cut the drive shaft to length, mount the crank, and you are ready to operate. The washing-machine transmission is constructed to create a back-and-forth motion by rotating the driveshaft. If you want to be very sophisticated and make the work very easy, instead of the crank, mount a small pulley on the shaft and attach a foot treadle to it. You can then churn your butter while your hands are busy doing other things.

CHAPTER 7

The Sap Is Running

In the early days of spring when the nights are cold but the days are warm with a westerly breeze blowing, the maple sap starts to run. Usually this happens in the middle of March, but it can happen as early as the middle of February.

Maple syrup is not only the first crop of the year on the farm, but it is also a family outing. It is something that has to be experienced — the feeling you get when you hear the fire snapping under the cauldron of the evaporator, then, after a short while, enjoying the sweet aroma that fills the sugar house. The best trees to tap are the sugar maple and the black maple.

When you first see your sugar bush, you think it will look after itself, but this is far from the case. To get the maximum amount of good-quality syrup from the sugar bush requires quite a lot of care. Consult the government forestry representative in your area for advice and guidance. A good, producing bush should contain from 40 to 50 sugar maple trees at least 9 inches in diameter measured at breast level. The maple tree, like any other tree, needs room to grow and to develop a spreading crown. Trees with full crowns produce more sap of a better quality, because they shade the ground below them, protecting it from drying out and stopping the leaf litter and humus from getting killed. The sap is composed largely of water so the amount of sap you get depends largely on the moisture in the ground. Keep the bush well trimmed, and cut down all soft wood growth such as pine, hemlock, spruce, and fir. Leave other hardwoods if they are needed to help retain a closed crown cover, but as young maples mature, thin out other hardwoods.

EQUIPMENT

As the date of the sap run is so unpredictable, it is wise to have all your equipment scrubbed and scalded and ready to go on a moment's notice as the first run of sap gives the best-quality syrup.

If you plan to tap for your own use only, a small number of trees close to the house may be tapped, and the sap may be boiled on the kitchen stove or outside in a large cauldron. But if a large quantity of sap is to be boiled, you must have an evaporator and a sugaring house.

TAPPING AUGER This is a short, coarse-threaded, sharp screw which cuts into the tree rapidly and smoothly. The size should be ⅜-inch in diameter, which allows a 7/16-inch sap spout to be driven into the hole to seal any leak.

SAP SPOUTS Most people prefer a metal spout which is easily cleaned and will not rust or corrode. The end of the spout should be rounded, smooth, and tapered; sturdy enough to be driven into the tree with a wooden mallet. The spout requires a hook on which the sap bucket will hang.

BUCKETS AND COVERS Buckets may be metal or plastic containers with a capacity of 8 to 10 quarts. They should be light and easy to clean and should stack for storage.

Bucket covers are recommended to prevent dirt, snow, and rain from dropping into the sap. Covers also keep the sap cool which is very important since sap will sour quickly if exposed to the heat from the sun.

GATHERING PAILS The gathering pails should be cone-shaped and made of galvanized steel. They should hold at least 16 to 18 quarts. The sap-gatherer needs two pails, one in each hand to balance his load.

GATHERING TANK The galvanized steel tank should have a capacity of 80 to 100 gallons which is just about right for a 200-tree operation. It should be equipped with a splash guard, a strainer on top, and an outlet pipe in the bottom. The tank is usually mounted on a sled or other low vehicle and is drawn through the bush by a horse or tractor.

STORAGE TANK This tank, also galvanized, should be placed close to the sugaring house and elevated to a height higher than the evaporator. It is desirable that the tank be kept on the north side of the sugaring house to keep the sap as cold as possible. It should hold at least 500 gallons but 700 or 800-gallon tanks are not unusual. The storage tank should be roofed.

100

SUGARING HOUSE This building is the heart of the operation and should be at least 20 feet long and 10 feet wide with a roof height of about 8 feet. If possible, build it close to a good water supply, and down grade from the sugar bush. A shed with enough space to hold at least two cords of firewood should be built at the end of the sugaring house near the door.

EVAPORATOR A series of low shallow pans connected to each other with tubes and equipped with baffles and placed on top of a firebox make up the evaporator. It is designed to reduce the maple sap to syrup with the least possible loss of time and heat. The faster this process takes place, the lighter in color the product.

FILTERS It is important that the hot syrup be filtered when it leaves the evaporator. Filters made out of heavy felt will remove sediment and impurities from the hot syrup.

THERMOMETERS To get a top-quality product a thermometer is necessary. It gives the proper boiling point of the syrup. Another handy gadget is a *hydrometer* to check the density of the syrup.

ODDS AND ENDS Skimming scoops are needed to skim the scum off the sap in the evaporator container. An old-style hand wringer to put the filters through after they have been washed is useful.

Now this does seem like a lot of equipment, but if you intend to go into making maple syrup for sale, this is what you need.

If you only intend to make enough for your own use all you really need is a ⅜-inch bit, a carpenter's brace, spouts, sap buckets or ordinary pails, a sugar thermometer, a large kettle or cauldron, and enough cans or bottles to hold the finished syrup.

Set a spout into a tree close to your home and (in the spring) check it daily. As soon as the sap starts running drill holes in the trees you intend to tap and collect the sap. Pour it immediately into your cauldron set over a hot fire. Boil until the thermometer registers the proper degree (it is marked on the thermometer) or, as my friend and neighbor, a veteran sugar-maker, Raymond Free told me "Dip the scoop into the syrup, hold it up, and let the syrup slowly drip off the scoop. When the sugar forms a light film hanging on the lip of the scoop the size of a silver dollar, it is time to draw it off."

Checking more than 100 batches, he was not out even by one quarter of a degree on any one of them.

TAPPING THE TREES

Never tap a tree that is less than 9 inches in diameter. A good rule is that trees from 9 to 15 inches in diameter take one bucket; 15 to 20-inch sizes can have two buckets (drill holes on opposite sides of the trunk); 21 to 25-inch trees support three buckets and those over 26 inches, four buckets. Another trick Raymond taught me is to "look overhead at the crown of the tree, drill your hole right under the heaviest branch of the tree, and you will get more sap."

Trees should be tapped 4 feet above the ground at a point where the bark is healthy. Avoid drilling in old tapping holes. If the scar in the bark from an old hole is still visible, move 10 inches to one side. Bore 2 to 2½ inches deep, slant the hole slightly upwards so that the sap will have a downhill path to the bucket. Clean the hole and drive the spout in firmly so that it will seal properly. Hang the bucket from the hook on the spout, cover the bucket, and wait.

The flow of sap is greatest between 9:00 a.m. and noon, but after an extremely cold night you might have to wait until early afternoon or even until just before dark. Sap flow changes from year to year, and cold days may cut off the flow altogether. Buckets should be emptied at least once a day. If the flow is heavy you might have to empty them twice a day. Do not throw away the ice that forms in the buckets overnight; put it into the gathering tank and it will help keep the sap cold.

The Indians used the freezing method to get rid of the water in the sap, by throwing away the ice on top of their containers and re-freezing it until they had a reasonably good product left in the bottom of the container.

OPERATING THE EVAPORATOR

Follow the manufacturer's instructions as closely as possible. If you have a second-hand evaporator and no instructions, here is a general guideline for most evaporators.

Before you start the fire under the pans, make sure that the sap flows freely through the regulating valve from the outside storage tank. It is extremely important that it operate properly and not let the sap overflow the pans.

The bottoms of the pans should be covered with 1½ to 2 inches of sap. After checking all valves, start your fire. As the sap starts to boil on the first intake, the sap from the syrup end of the pan (the end pan) should be "dipped back" to the first pan until the desired density of the syrup has been reached.

From time to time you have to skim off the scum as it forms on top of the syrup. As the sap boils down, it should be kept flowing steadily from compartment to compartment. Never at any time let the pans boil dry. If the sap flow slows down, shut down the operation in plenty of time to ensure that the pans remain partly full. If you have a hydrometer, the BAUME reading for finished syrup is 36° at 60°. Syrup should weigh 11 to 11½ pounds per gallon. It takes approximately 40 gallons of sap to produce 1 gallon of syrup.

After the syrup has been drawn from the evaporator, is should be filtered as hot as possible through a felt strainer. Two filters are useful; when one is in use the other can be hung over the evaporator to allow all the syrup contained in the felt to drain out before being thoroughly washed.

MAPLE SYRUP PRODUCTS

It is essential when making maple-syrup products that your sugar thermometer read correctly. Since thermometers are graduated at sea level, you must determine the correct reading at your level. The simplest way to do this is to bring a pot of snow to a boil. Insert a thermometer into the boiling water, read it, and add seven degrees for each 1,000 feet of elevation. This will give you the proper boiling point of syrup.

Maple Syrup on Snow

A favorite of both young and old during the sugaring season is maple syrup on snow. Place the hot syrup from the evaporator into a smaller pot and reheat the syrup to 40° F above the boiling point of water. Without stirring it, pour it on the snow. The rapidly cooled syrup turns into a taffy-like sheet of candy without crystallizing.

Maple Sugar

The early settlers often made much of their maple syrup into hard maple sugar. The sugar was a more convenient form in which to store the sweetener during the long months before their supply could be replenished.

Long before the white man came to this continent the Indians knew how to make hard maple sugar, as the carved wooden molds bear witness. Often small birchbark canoes were made and filled with maple sugar, another convenient way of storing the sugar.

The sugar is easy to make. Heat syrup in a small container to 45°F above the boiling point of water. When it starts to thicken, remove it from the heat and stir with a wooden spoon until it starts to crystallize and stiffen. Pour into molds or wooden forms for storage.

Maple Butter

Maple butter resembles butter in texture and spreads easily on bread. It was often made on the homestead and used as a substitute for butter. The first requirement for maple butter is that only the best fresh maple syrup be used.

In a large kettle, heat the syrup to a temperature of 23-24° F above the boiling point of water. As soon as the syrup reaches the correct temperature, remove it from the heat quickly to prevent crystallization. Use a large, flat-bottomed pan immersed in ice-water. Pour boiling syrup in the pan to a depth of 1½ inches, never more. You may have to add crushed ice to the water-pan so that it can be cooled to about 50° F as fast as possible. Pour the chilled, thickened syrup into a large flat pan. Working with two hardwood paddles, about 3 inches wide, with sharp edges, scrape the thick syrup with the paddles from one side to the other, changing paddles frequently. If you have an old batch of maple syrup, add one teaspoonful of it to a gallon of cooked syrup and you will cut the creaming process time in half. (Starting from scratch it normally takes about 2 hours to produce the butter.) Store in wide-mouthed glass jars and refrigerate until used.

Maple Fluff

This product resembles maple butter but is much easier to make. Often the lower-quality, darker maple syrup is used. Heat the syrup to a temperature of 17° F above that of boiling water. Allow it to cool, stirring only occasionally until the sugar thermometer registers between 175° and 185° F. Add ⅓ cup of purified monoglycerine (purchased from a drugstore) per gallon of syrup, a little at a time and stir constantly until it has thoroughly dissolved in the hot syrup. Cool to a temperature of between 150 and 160°F and, using a household beater at high speed, quickly whip the mixture. It should become fluffy within 2 minutes. Store in a glass jar and refrigerate.

104

COOKING WITH MAPLE SYRUP

Maple Sugar Candy

1 cup sugar
1 cup maple syrup
½ cup sweet cream

½ cup cold water
2 tablespoons butter

Place all the ingredients in a 2-quart saucepan and bring to a boil. Test the mixture from time to time by dropping one drop into cold water. When the mixture holds together, remove from heat and stir until it thickens. Pour on a buttered cookie sheet and, while still warm, score into squares with a buttered knife.

Maple Fudge

1 quart maple syrup   1 cup sweet cream

Put the syrup and cream into a 2-quart saucepan and bring to a boil. Cook until it forms a hard ball when dropped into cold water. Remove from heat and cool. When cold stir until it hardens. Pour on a greased cookie sheet and score with a buttered knife.

Maple Syrup Pie

Grandmom's Pie Crust

1 pound lard
1 cup boiling water
¼ teaspoon salt

¼ teaspoon baking powder
6 cups all-purpose flour

Let the lard sit overnight at room temperature to soften. In a large mixing bowl, cream the lard with a fork and add the boiling water, making sure that the lard has completely dissolved. Add the salt and baking powder; stir well. Add 5 cups of the flour, one at a time; mix well with a fork or your hands into a smooth dough. If necessary for the proper consistency, add part of the sixth cup a little at a time. Do not over-work the dough. Chill and refrigerate at least one hour before using. Roll out as thin as possible on a baking board. Makes 4 single crusts.

Filling

1½ cups maple syrup
1 cup sugar
4 egg yolks

½ cup butter
½ teaspoon nutmeg
4 egg whites

Line a 9-inch pie plate with pie crust and set aside. In a mixing bowl cream the butter and half the sugar until fluffy. Add the beaten egg yolks, maple syrup, and nutmeg. Stir well. Pour the filling into the pie crust and bake in a medium-hot oven (350°-375°F) for 30 minutes.

Remove from oven and cool. Beat the 4 egg whites and the rest of the sugar until fluffy. Spread over top of the pie and bake again until light brown.

Maple Sponge Cake

11 egg yolks	2¼ cups sifted cake flour
2 cups maple syrup	2 teaspoons baking powder
1 cup scalded milk	½ cup melted butter
½ teaspoon lemon	¼ teaspoon salt
½ teaspoon vanilla	

Beat egg yolks with the maple syrup until very fluffy and light in color. Add the scalded milk a little at a time so the egg yolks do not cook. Add flavoring. Sift flour, salt, and baking powder three times and add to mixture. Carefully fold in butter. Turn into 3 greased layer-cake pans lined with waxed paper and greased again. Bake in a 350°F oven for about 25 minutes.

Maple Frosting and Filling

2 cups broken and rolled maple sugar	1 cup cream

Place the cream and sugar in a 2-quart saucepan and boil until a drop hardens in cold water (about 50 minutes). Remove from heat and cool slightly; beat until creamy and soft. Spread between layers and on top and sides of cake. If you want heavy glazing, double the recipe.

Maple Sugar Cookies

3 cups flour	2 eggs
1 teaspoon salt	1½ cups maple sugar,
½ teaspoon soda	crushed and rolled
1 teaspoon baking powder	½ teaspoon vanilla
½ cup lard	½ teaspoon almond extract
½ cup butter	

Sift together flour, salt, soda, and baking powder. Cut in buttter and lard as for pie crust. Beat eggs until light and gradually add maple sugar. Beat until mixture is very light and fiuffy, then add flavoring and continue beating. Combine the two mixtures and beat well again. Wrap in waxed paper and chill. Roll dough into small balls, place on cookie sheet, and indent with your thumb. Bake at 375°F until a delicate shade of gold.

Light Maple Syrup Bread

1 cup cornmeal	2 teaspoons cream of tartar
1¾ cups whole wheat flour	1 cup maple syrup
1 teaspoon salt	2 cups sour milk
1 teaspoon soda	

Mix the two flours, salt, soda, and cream of tartar. Add the maple syrup to the milk, pour over the dry ingredients and mix well. Grease a 1½-quart bread mold and fill with the mixture. Bake in a 325°F oven for 1 hour. Cool on cake rack. Serve warm.

Maple Syrup Toast

6 slices whole wheat bread	1½ cups maple sugar
butter	crushed and rolled

Toast the bread on one side. Butter the untoasted side. Sprinkle the crushed and rolled sugar generously over the butter. Arrange on a cookie sheet and place under broiler until sugar melts. Serve in a bowl with cream.

CHAPTER 8

The Bees Are Here

As soon as the snow melted we started to look for a suitable place for our apiary, as we had ordered four 3-pound packages of bees that were due to arrive early in the spring. During the winter months we had labored hard to make the hives and frames for our colonies; now the time had come to select a place to put them.

Bees should be located where they get the morning and evening sun, but where they have light shade from 10 a.m. to 3 p.m. The hives should face east or south, and have adequate shelter from cold westerly and northerly winds. They should be placed well away from buildings and not near clotheslines or other places frequented daily by people or livestock. Consider the place carefully so that the hives do not have to be moved once they are set in place and the bees have established themselves.

GETTING READY FOR THE BEES

Using blocks, bricks, or pieces of wood, make a stand for each hive. It must be high enough so the hive will always be out of water. Tilt the hive slightly forward so that water and moisture can run off the entrance but make sure it is reasonably level crosswise. Place the hives approximately 3 feet apart and cut the grass in front of the hives. Leave enough space behind the hives so that you can get at them easily because they are worked from the back. It is also handy if you have enough room near your hives to, at a later time, erect the honey-house, in which to store the extractor and the unused hives. The honey-house should be dry and all joints should be well caulked so that the bees cannot get into it when you are extracting the honey in the fall. I put an old wood-stove in the house to keep it warm during the honey-extracting season. Also it is a handy place to heat water when mixing sugar-syrup.

Buy 25 pounds of white granulated sugar for each package of bees, and even before they arrive, prepare a sugar syrup (one pint per swarm) in the proportion of 10 pounds of sugar to 1 gallon of warm water.

After the hives have been placed on the stands, remove half of the frames and foundations to leave yourself enough space in the middle to pour the packaged bees. Place a Boardman feeder in the entrance and shove some grass or weeds loosely into the opening. Do not pack the opening air-tight but just tightly enough that the bees cannot get out easily.

Order your bees for an early spring delivery; early in April is best. If it should be snowing or raining when they arrive, have no fear, because they can be kept in their cage for several days.

BEEKEEPING EQUIPMENT

At this point let us talk about the tools and equipment you will need in addition to the hives. Bee stings are annoying, but the degree of sensitivity varies considerably. Bees seem less likely to sting people wearing light-colored clothing. Therefore you should purchase a *white coverall* with long sleeves and long pants that can be tucked into your boots; the sleeves should be long enough to reach well under elbow-length *cotton gloves*. The gloves should have plastic-covered hands and elasticized tops. A *fiber helmet* equipped with a canvas-bound veil will protect your face and neck. A *bee-smoker* is a must to drive the bees down into their hive when checking the frames for queen cells or comb burring. A steel *hive tool* is also necessary to pry loose the frames from the body.

All beginners should use *queen excluders*. The queen excluder is an accurately spaced screen placed above the brood nest. The worker bees are small enough to pass through it but the queen and the drones are excluded from the supers above. The use of the excluder is hotly debated by beekeepers but I recommend them at least until you are able to recognize the queen. Otherwise, when you remove the supers you might accidentally also remove the queen. If you do use an excluder, remember to remove it late in the summer to allow the bees to store honey and pollen in all available combs.

These are the supplies the beginner needs to be able to work comfortably with his bees; all can be purchased from a bee-supply house.

BEEKEEPING

Success with even a few colonies requires a thorough knowledge of the life and behavior of bees. This knowledge can best be obtained by

110

experience. If you have the opportunity to work with a skilled bee-keeper, this is the ideal situation. Even if you have to work for no pay, the experience you get will be well worth it. Read the best books on the market and subscribe to a good bee journal and your ability to take care of your bees will gradually increase.

One balmy mid-April day the expected phone call came, announcing that my bees had arrived. I was busy, so a friend offered to get them. Late in the afternoon he arrived with four cages of wildly buzzing bees, some loose bees flying around in his car, and a panic-stricken wife. I dropped everything and rushed to my bees. The first job was to feed them. When they first arrive, feed each swarm a pint or more of the sugar syrup, and then set them in the shade for one hour so that they can clean up all the syrup and calm down a bit before you attempt to install them in the hive. Each cage contains several thousand bees; a small box of bees containing the queen comes separately.

Remove the queen's cage and find the queen who is longer and slim-mer than the other bees. Do not worry about her small size as she has not been laying eggs for several days; once she is introduced to the hive and begins laying she will be about three times as large. It is most important that she be alive and healthy. A sure way to tell the queen from the workers is by the middle part of her body to which the legs and wings are attached. It is bald and shiny, while this part of the worker and drone bees is covered with short, downy hairs.

Now remove the cork or paper from the ⅜-inch hole in the candy end of the queen's cage and hang it, candy end down, between the sec-ond and third frames (supporting it with a wire wrapped around a small nail driven in the top bar). Make sure that the candy end is open so that the bees (within a few hours) can chew through it and release the queen. Sprinkle each package with a quart of cold water. Do not be afraid of drowning your bees and do not be afraid of wetting them down too much. In extremely hot weather more cold water may be re-quired to drive them off the screen and to make them cluster tightly. (Sprinkling with water makes them easier to handle and will stop them from flying.) Now jam the shipping cage firmly to the ground and remove the feeder can; then pour the bees into the opening in your hive made by the five frames removed previously.

Leave the hives alone for a couple of days, then remove the cover and replace the five frames that you removed earlier. Check your feeder every day and add syrup if needed. The feeding should be continued until the bees have completely drawn out all of the frames in the brood nest and have filled them with honey and brood. After about a week remove the frames one by one and check them to make sure the queen is laying eggs. Also at this time try to locate the queen; you will see that she is about double the size she was when she arrived. With the queen laying eggs and the feeder constantly full of syrup, you will notice eggs in some cells and horseshoe-shaped larvae in others.

To work with your bees in comfort you have to use the smoker to open and enter the hives. Never use silk, wool, or hair for smoker fuel, as it burns with an odor and will make the bees cross. Cotton or burlap bagging, or punk (decayed) wood are good, but I have found that the flower structure from the staghorn sumac gives by far the best and coolest smoke. Light the smoker with a piece of paper and work the bellows until you have a thick, cool smoke emitting from the pipe of the smoker.

Approach the hives from behind, reach around to the front, and send 5 or 6 good puffs of smoke into the entrance. This will run the guards into the hive and many bees will put their heads in the cells and fill themselves with honey.

Always remember when working with bees not to make any quick movements, or to block the entranceway for the field bees coming home heavily loaded with pollen and nectar. Never jar a hive as this will anger the bees. Pry the supers and the frames apart with a steady pressure of your hive tool rather than with a quick movement.

Carefully lift one corner of the cover and blow a couple of puffs of smoke down into the hive. Now, with the hive tool in one hand and the smoker in the other, pry off the inner cover, lift it up on one side, and blow smoke down under the cover, forcing the bees into the hive.

When the brood chamber is getting full you should place a super on top of the brood chamber. You must give the bees room to work and empty combs to fill, otherwise they will swarm and you will lose honey. It is advisable to use only 9 frames in a 10-frame body. Check daily to see how the bees are coming along. When you notice that the middle frames in the super are getting fully drawn out and filled with honey, they should be moved toward the outside and the empty outer frames moved in to the center of the super.

When the super is full, lift it off the brood chamber and replace it with an empty super. Place the nearly full super on top and replace the inner cover and the telescopic cover again. The reason for replacing the nearly full super is because bees need time to evaporate and condense the nectar, which is as thin as water when it is first introduced in the cells. Always remember to place the fresh super next to the brood chamber and the nearly full one on top to give the bees a chance to complete the work of evaporation and of capping the cells.

112

"How often do you rob your bees?" is an often-asked question. Of course you never rob your bees or they will starve. Never remove any honey without first making sure that the bees have ample stores until the next honey flow. I usually leave all my supers on the hive until the season is over. Sometimes this will leave me with hives six or seven stories high.

Make sure that all the frames are capped before you remove them. The bees are experts in their trade and, if the cells are not capped, the honey is probably still thin and needs additional evaporation and processing before the experts put the seal of approval on the cell.

HARVESTING THE HONEY

All during the summer's honey flow you will have the pleasure of watching the honey increase but there comes a time when you must harvest what has been gathered. First find a suitable room free from foreign odors. The room should be as airtight as possible, well lighted, and heatable to at least 75°F. (Honey is easier to extract at this temperature.) Place all your supers criss-crossed on top of each other and let them sit for at least 24 hours.

The first chore is to uncap the frames. This can be done either with a special electric knife or with an ordinary knife that has been heated in hot water. I have found the extra cost of an electric, heated knife well worth it. To uncap a comb of honey, start at either the bottom or the top of the comb and, with a back-and-forth sawing movement, cut off the cappings. Use the bottom and the top bars as guides and take a deep cut which is sure to get all of the cappings at one pass. The uncapping should be done over a tub which has a screen about halfway up from the bottom. The cappings will fall down on the screen and the honey in the caps will drain to the bottom of the tub.

Now, if you are lucky enough to have a honey extractor, the frames are simply placed in this instrument which works on the centrifugal principle and, when set in motion, either by a hand crank or an electric motor, rotates the frames, forcing the honey out of the cells, towards the walls of the extractor. The honey gradually drains to the bottom and from there it is drawn off into suitable containers.

If you do not have an extractor, the honey can still be extracted but much more slowly. The combs have to be smashed and heat has to be applied to separate the honey from the wax. The disadvantage with this process is that the combs are destroyed and you have to start from the beginning every spring, consequently a great deal of the bees' time is lost in making new combs every year.

COOKING WITH HONEY

Honey is a high-energy carbohydrate food. Honey and maple sugar were by far the most-used sweeteners by the early settlers to this continent.

Honey adds flavor to baking, and also gives baked goods a moist texture so that they remain palatable for a longer period than similar sugar-based products.

Honey may be substituted as the sweetening agent in any recipe calling for sugar. In muffins, breads, and rolls calling for a small amount of sugar, honey can replace the sugar measure for measure without any adjustment. For cakes and cookies that require a large amount of sugar, honey still can be used measure for measure, but the amount of liquid must be reduced by ¼ cup for each cup of honey used. Always bake in a moderate oven (350° to 375°F) to prevent the product becoming too brown.

Mead

You often hear about honey wine but this is a misnomer as the drink made out of honey is mead. Mead was possibly man's first alcoholic drink. It was made in India thousands of years ago, and was a great favorite of the Vikings.

In an old roadside inn just outside the university town of Upsala in Sweden, mead is still served in inlaid silver tankards made of cows' horns, in the old Viking way. Here is the recipe as given to me by the innkeeper. It dates back to the early days of the inn, about 650 A.D.

1½ pounds honey	1 tablespoon cardamom, crushed
1 quart boiling water	1 tablespoon cloves, crushed
2 bottles of stout	1 tablespoon whole ginger, crushed
or porter	

Bring the water to a rolling boil in a 2-quart saucepan. Add the cardamom, cloves, and the crushed ginger; remove from heat, and cool to room temperature. Strain and then dissolve the honey in the water. Add the stout or porter, mixing well. Store in a cool place but do not chill. When ready to use, warm on the stove to slightly above room temperature.

Sweet Fried Cakes in Honey Syrup

4 cups wheat flour
1 teaspoon salt
2 teaspoons baking powder
4 eggs
4 tablespoons rendered beef fat
    for frying

½ cup honey
water or milk
1 pound rendered beef fat

Sift flour and salt with baking powder. Cut 4 tablespoons of the fat into the flour mixture. Beat eggs and honey; add flour mixture. Add enough water or milk to make a medium dough, neither stiff nor soft. Let dough stand for ½ hour. Roll out on floured board to ¼-inch thick, cut into 1½-inch squares and fry in deep fat until brown.

Honey Syrup

2 cups honey
½ cup water

2 teaspoons cinnamon

Place the honey in a 1-quart saucepan; add the water and heat slowly, stirring constantly. When the honey mixture starts to thicken, add the cinnamon and mix well. Remove from heat and cool. Dip sweet fried cakes in the syrup and serve hot.

Honey-Glazed Carrots

1½ pounds new carrots
1 bouillion cube
1¼ cups water

3 tablespoons honey
4 tablespoons margarine

Scrape and wash carrots. Dissolve bouillion cube in water; add margarine and honey. Simmer carrots in this mixture until soft. Remove the carrots and cook sauce until reduced and thick. Put carrots back in and coat them with the sauce by shaking over low heat. Serve as vegetable with any meat.

Whole Fried Wild Onions in Honey

10 wild onions
2 cups water
2 tablespoons butter

1 tablespoon honey
salt and pepper

Peel and boil onions in lightly salted water for 10 minutes. Drain and save 1 cup onion stock. Brown butter and honey in a cast-iron frying pan, add the onions, and sprinkle salt and pepper on top to taste. Shake the pan to turn the onions. Add the onion stock. Cover and simmer for 30 minutes. Serve with roast lamb or mutton.

Stewed Wild Asparagus in Honey

1 pound wild asparagus tips	2 tablespoons butter
2 cups water	1 tablespoon flour
1 bouillon cube	2 tablespoons honey

Clean and was the wild asparagus tips. Dissolve bouillon cube in the water; add honey and asparagus tips. Simmer until tips are soft, but just underdone. Melt butter in another saucepan and add flour. Add cooking fluid gradually while stirring and cook until thick and smooth. Add asparagus tips and let mixture come to a boil. Season to taste. Serve with any wild meat.

Pot Roast with Wine and Honey

1 4 to 5-pound sirloin-tip roast	5 small carrots, washed and
1 tablespoon salt	scraped
1 teaspoon pepper	1 cup red wine
4 small onions	1 cup honey

Wash the meat. Rub salt and pepper all over it. In a large, iron frying pan sear the meat on all sides until dark brown. Add to a Dutch oven the wine and honey, well mixed. Put the quartered onions and carrots on the bottom of the pot, and the meat on top. Cover and simmer until meat is tender. Remove the meat and strain the juices into a smaller pot. Mix flour and water to a thick paste; add to gravy until desired thickness. Just before serving, add 1 tablespoon of brandy.

Hasenpfeffer in Honey

1 rabbit, cut into serving pieces	12 whole cloves
3 tablespoons salt	flour, salt, and pepper
2 quarts water	1 cup lard
1 large onion	1 cup honey

Mix the salt and water in a stainless steel bowl, add the pieces of rabbit, and let stand for 4 hours. Rinse in cold water. Pierce the onion and set the whole cloves into it. Put the rabbit, onion, and water in a

116

3-quart saucepan and cook until tender. Mix the flour, salt, and pepper on a plate and roll the rabbit meat in the flour mixture taking care that each piece is well coated. Melt the lard and the honey in a heavy skillet. When hot, fry the rabbit meat until brown. Lower the heat, cover the skillet, and simmer for 30 minutes. Remove the rabbit meat and keep warm. Add a little flour to the cooking fluids in the skillet and make a gravy. Serve hot with the gravy poured over the meat.

Honey-Stuffed Baked Apples

8 large cooking apples	2 tablespoons water
4 tablespoons ground almonds	3 tablespoons butter
5 tablespoons honey	1 tablespoon ginger

Mix honey with almonds and water. Wash and dry apples. Remove cores but leave apples whole. With a fork, prick the apples all over. Stuff honey mixture into the center of the apples; coat with melted, slightly cooled butter; sprinkle ginger on top. Place in a buttered, shallow baking pan. Bake in moderate oven for about 1 hour. Baste the apples from time to time with the cooking fluids. Serve warm with whipped cream.

Honey Coffee Cake

4 cups all-purpose flour	½ teaspoon salt
1 cup butter	1 egg
1 package yeast	1¼ cups cream
2 tablespoons honey	

Garnish

1 egg, beaten	15 chopped almonds
3 tablespoons sugar	icing sugar and water glaze
1 tablespoon cinnamon	

Mix yeast with a little sugar and set aside. Place two thirds of the flour in a mixing bowl and cut buttter into it. Mix honey, salt, cream, and egg; add the yeast. Work in the rest of the flour. Butter a baking dish and flatten dough to fit. Set aside to rise for 45 minutes. Brush with beaten egg and sprinkle with sugar, cinnamon, and chopped almonds. Bake in 400°F oven until golden. Glaze with icing sugar and water. Cut into squares and serve hot.

117

Soft Brown Honey Cake

2 eggs
6 tablespoons butter
2 cups honey
1½ cups self-rising flour

2 teaspoons cinnamon
1 teaspoon ground cardamom
½ cup sour cream
breadcrumbs

Butter one cake pan and sprinkle with bread crumbs. Melt butter and cool. Beat eggs and honey until light and fluffy; stir in seasonings and the melted butter; add the sour cream. Stir in flour a little at a time. Pour into pan and bake in moderate oven for about 45 minutes. Let cool in pan.

RECOMMENDED READING

The Hive and the Honey Bee, Dadant & Sons, Hamilton, Illinois
How to Keep Bees and Sell Honey, The Walter T. Kelly Co., Clarkson, Kentucky.

CHAPTER 9

Chickens, Ducks, and Geese

What is the earliest date of poultry keeping? Nobody knows. But we do know that eggs and fowl are an important part of our daily diet. On a homestead, far away from the stores, you realize just how important eggs and birds are in your diet.

As eggs do not keep well in non-refrigerated storage, it soon dawns on you that it is important to you and your family to acquire a flock of chickens, ducks, and, maybe, a couple of geese.

CHICKEN COOPS

A flock of 50 to 100 chickens will keep the average household in eggs and eating birds all-year around. A chicken coop is fairly inexpensive and is easy to construct. Build one as soon as possible. Utility American and English birds require a floor space of about 3 square feet and about 8 inches roosting space. Less space and the flock is open to disease and cannibalism and will not lay well.

The climate in the chicken coop is also important. The coop should be dry and free from drafts with adequate ventilation. Good ventilation can be obtained by leaving one side of the house open. The open side should face away from the prevailing winds. The temperature inside the coop should never be allowed to rise above 75°F. Chickens can stand several degrees of frost but temperatures above 75° cause the birds to become irritable. They will peck one another, especially during the moulting season (chickens have three a year).

Lighting is another important factor. The birds should have about 12 hours of light a day, preferably natural light. Birds, as all animals, are

119

CHICKEN HOUSE

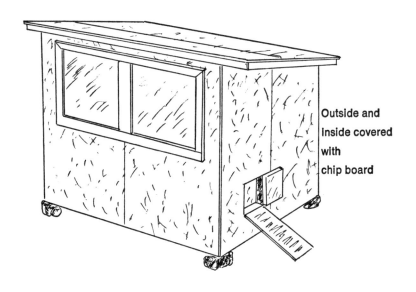

Outside and inside covered with chip board

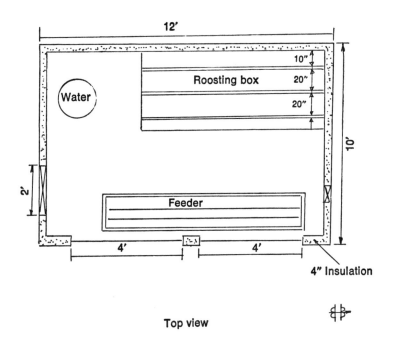

Top view

regular in their habits and an extensive variation in the hours of light will affect the production of eggs. Unless you can rigidly control artificial light, it is better to depend on natural light alone.

Inside the chicken house you will need roosting bars and a platform called a drop board. The roosting bars should be made out of 2 x 2s and placed horizontally, above and parallel to the drop board. The first bar should be placed about 10 inches from the wall, and subsequent bars 20 inches away from the first one. The drop board should be about 30 inches above the floor of the coop, and the roosts 6 to 8 inches above the drop board. This makes it more convenient for cleaning. I place a thin layer of peat moss on the drop board and when it has become mixed with the droppings I store the mixture in empty feed sacks, to be used for plants requiring a high nitrogen fertilizer.

The birds require a large exercise yard — a good rule of thumb is to allow 5 square feet per bird. The yard can be constructed of chicken wire, and should be located either on the east or west side of the building. A southern exposure usually does not provide the birds with enough shade during the day.

CHICKENS

When you have the housing problem solved you must decide how to start your flock. One way is to buy day-old chicks, but as very young chicks require a lot of care and must be kept in a heated brooder house, it is usually more convenient to buy older chicks or pullets almost ready to lay. Buy only from a reputable breeder; be sure that the chicks have been tested and are free from disease.

If you have acquired 8-to-10-week-old chickens you can start them on an all-mash growing diet, or a combination of growing mash and grain. Start with a small amount of grain and increase it gradually until the birds are getting equal parts of mash and grain. I use 2½ pounds of crushed corn and 2½ pounds of laying mash mixed with 2 tablespoons of cod liver oil for 15 chickens. Grit and oystershell are necessary to supply the calcium required for normal eggshells.

If you feed and care for your laying hens carefully, you should get high-quality eggs for your family, and occasionally you may have a surplus to sell.

Gather eggs from the nests twice daily; clean and cool them. Eggs should be stored at a temperature between 45° and 55°F. If you are selling eggs, build up a good reputation by not including small or thin-shelled eggs.

DUCKS AND GEESE

Well-fleshed, moderately fat geese and ducks provide nutritious and tasty food. Rearing waterfowl under proper conditions is not difficult, but before attempting to do so as a source of income investigate the processing and marketing aspects of this industry. If you only wish to raise these fowl for your own use, it is quite simple. Ducks and geese require less care and attention than chickens and the only housing they need is some type of shelter from the wind. Geese can also save you hours of back-breaking labor. They will eat weeds in your strawberry and asparagus patches and in the orchard. For successful weeding, goslings should not be over six-weeks old, as older stock is more likely to injure plants and fruits. Weeder goslings must be kept hungry, or they will not work. However, a light feed of grain or complete pelleted mash is usually necessary at night. Good shade and running water are essential for both ducks and geese.

White Pekin, Rouen, and Muscovy are the ducks usually selected for meat production with the Pekin being the most popular. The most popular geese breeds are Embden, Toulouse, and White Chinese. A cross between the large Chinese male and the medium-sized Embden female usually results in fast-growing goslings, mainly white in color in both sexes, and of a good market type and size.

SOME UNUSUAL EGG RECIPES

The fresher eggs are, the better they taste. An easy way to tell a good egg from a bad one is to place the egg in a container of water. The good ones will lie on their sides; those that turn with the large end upward are bad and should be rejected.

When eggs are plentiful they may be preserved in several ways. An old method is to pack the eggs in salt, being careful that the eggs do not touch each other. Another old method is to dip the eggs in wax or rub them with lard, then pack them in bran or oats. In the latter part of the 19th century waterglass (sodium silicate) was used for preserving eggs. The waterglass was mixed with water in the proportion of 1 quart of waterglass to 1 gallon of water, the mixture was then put in a large stone crock, and the eggs were added.

When breaking eggs, they should be broken separately over a cup, to ensure perfection. In the old days the shells were washed, and saved for settling coffee.

Three minutes will boil an egg soft; five minutes will cook the white hard but not the yolk; eight to ten minutes will cook it hard clear through — hard enough to slice or serve with salads.

It has been claimed that there are over six-hundred different ways to serve eggs, but I am including only a few dating back to the early days of the settlers.

Baked Eggs

Break 8 eggs in a bowl, add 3 tablespoons of cream, salt and pepper to taste; beat well. Grease large cocoa cups well with butter. Pour the milk-egg mixture into the cups until three-quarters full. Place on a cookie sheet and bake at 350°F for about 20 minutes. Serve from the cups with a piece of toast.

Creamed Eggs

Grease an individual egg pan; break the egg carefully into it. Put small pieces of buttter, and a tablespoon of cream over each egg. Season with salt and pepper; bake for about 5 minutes and the egg is done.

Egg Gems

Mix together 2½ cups of bread crumbs and 2½ cups of chopped, cooked meat; season with salt and pepper and a little butter; moisten with a little milk or water. Heat the mixture thoroughly. Fill patty pans with the mixture; break an egg on top of each, and bake until the eggs are cooked. (Cold roast beef or lean pork are especially good.)

Ox Eyes (Toad in the Hole — Hunter's Breakfast)

Cut 2-inch slices from a long, round loaf of bread; carefully remove a portion of the centre of each piece; place in a deep buttered dish. Beat 2 eggs with ¾ cup of milk; add salt and pepper and pour over the bread until all the fluid has been absorbed by the bread. Carefully break an egg into each cavity and bake in a hot oven until set.

Eggs in Tomatoes

Take medium-sized tomatoes (one for each serving); cut off the tops; scoop out the seeds, and break an egg into each shell. Season with salt and pepper and place a dab of buttter on top. Bake in a hot oven until set.

Egg-Nest Toast

Toast as many slices of bread as desired; dip quickly in salted water; butter, and put into a baking pan in a warm oven. Using one egg for each piece of toast, carefully separate the yolks from the whites; beat the whites into a stiff froth; place a spoonful on each slice of toast, making a dent in the middle to accommodate the yolk. Place the yolk in the indentation. Bake in a hot oven to brown lightly. Serve hot.

Cupped Eggs

Take the required number of large cocoa cups and put into each a spoonful of well-seasoned beef gravy. Place the cups in a pan of boiling water. When the gravy is hot, drop an egg into each cup; remove the pan from the heat; cover with aluminum foil and let stand until the eggs are cooked. Sprinkle with salt and pepper.

Stuffed Eggs

Cut 6 hard-boiled eggs in half; remove the yolks and mash them finely. Add 2 tablespoons cream, finely chopped anchovies, and salt and pepper. Mix well. Fill the whites with the mixture. Add a well-beaten egg to the left-over mixture, dip the eggs into this mixture, then roll them in cracker crumbs. Fry in hot fat until lightly browned.

Oven-Baked Omelet with Ham

A French chef once told me that there are as many ways to make omelets as there are chefs. Over a bottle of fine wine he let me in on the secret of making omelets. As his was one of the best I have ever tasted, I will also let you in on the secret.

Yolks should be lightly beaten with a fork. Too much beating will make the omelet too thin. He said that 12 beats is the magic number. Never use milk: one tablespoon of ice water for each egg is enough. Let stand for a few minutes when you beat the whites to a froth. Sprinkle salt and pepper to taste over the beaten yolks before you fold in the whites.

A lightly greased omelet skillet should be heated until the butter is lightly browned but not so hot that it scorches the butter. Slowly pour in the eggs — they should start to bubble and rise in flakes at once. Using a chilled fork, lift the omelet from the bottom occasionally to prevent burning. Fold over as soon as the underside is set enough to hold together. This is done by gently shaking the skillet. Slide it carefully onto a heated platter and serve at once.

If a filling is used, shake only half of the omelet over onto the platter: add the filling in the middle; then fold the rest of the omelet over the filling.

1 cup milk, boiling	1 teaspoon salt
6 eggs	½ teaspoon pepper
1 teaspoon cornstarch	1 tablespoon butter
1 cup ham, finely chopped	

Separate the eggs; place yolks in a mixing bowl; beat lightly. Pour the boiling milk over the yolks, stir in the cornstarch dissolved in a little cold milk, and beat in beaten egg whites. Add the chopped ham. Butter a baking dish well, pour in the egg-ham mixture, and bake in 350°F oven for 15 minutes or until well-browned on top. Serve with cranberry sauce.

SOME UNUSUAL POULTRY RECIPES

Clint Woodbeck Chicken Special

1 chicken, quartered	½ teaspoon pepper
½ teaspoon salt	1 cup mayonnaise

Wash and clean the chicken and quarter it. Sprinkle with salt and pepper. Completely cover each piece with mayonnaise and place on a rack in an oven pan. Bake in a preheated oven at 350°F for 1 hour. Baste occasionally with cooking fluids and, if necessary, add more mayonnaise. When tender, place the chicken under the broiler for a few minutes to brown on all sides.

Fried Spanish Chicken

1 frying chicken, cut into pieces	1 clove garlic, chopped
flour	1 sweet green pepper, chopped
½ cup butter	3 tablespoons flour
salt	1 cup water
2 tablespoons chopped onions	2 tablespoons lemon juice
2 tablespoons chopped parsley	

Dredge chicken in flour. Fry in buttter until brown; sprinkle with salt, remove from pan and keep warm. Fry onion, parsley, garlic, and green pepper in the butter. Brown the flour, add water, and cook until thick. Salt to taste and add lemon juice. Pour the sauce over the warm chicken and serve hot.

To Cook an Old Hen so It Will Be like a Young Chicken

Cut up chicken; dredge thickly with flour; place in a skillet with hot fat and butter and fry until nicely browned. Pour off excess fat; almost cover with water and bake for 2 hours or until tender. Keep some water in the pan until half an hour before chicken is done, then remove water and pour 1 cup rich sour cream over it. A rich gravy will be formed.

Goose Stuffed with Chestnuts

2½ pounds chestnuts	2 pounds pork, finely chopped
2 cups lard	1 tablespoon salt
1 cup consommé	1 teaspoon pepper
1 8-10 pound goose	

Make a cut in each chestnut shell. Heat lard in a 6 to 7-inch skillet until it smokes. Add the chestnuts and let them simmer for 1 minute; remove from fat; drain on paper towel and peel. In a 2-quart saucepan combine the consommé and the chestnuts; bring to a boil, lower the heat and cook until the chestnuts are tender. Add the chestnuts to the finely chopped pork and rub the mixture through a sieve. Fill the bird with this mixture, truss, and roast either on a spit or in the oven, basting frequently with melted butter or fat from the oven pan. Allow 20 minutes per pound at 325°F.

Roast Goose

1 10-12 pound goose, cleaned and dressed	2 oranges, chopped
1 large apple, chopped	1 cup celery, chopped

Stuffing

4 cups dry bread crumbs	½ teaspoon salt
3 cups apples, chopped	1 cup white wine
3 cups oranges, chopped	

Mixture for Basting

1 cup apple juice	1 cup melted butter
1 cup orange juice	

Wash the cleaned goose thoroughly and pat dry. Mix the chopped apples, oranges, and celery; place in the cavity and let stand overnight in a covered roasting pan in a cool place.

Mix the bread crumbs, chopped apples, oranges, salt, and the wine in a large mixing bowl. Remove the filling from the cavity and discard.

126

Fill the cavity with the stuffing. Close the cavity and truss the legs. Baste the bird with the basting mixture. Bake, uncovered, on a rack in the roasting pan in a preheated oven at 400°F for 15 minutes or until the bird is golden brown. Reduce the heat to 325°F, cover the roasting pan, and cook until tender, basting every 10 minutes with the basting fluid. Allow 20 minutes per pound, starting the timing after the first 30 minutes.

Gravy

3 tablespoons flour	1 teaspoon salt
½ cup red currant jelly	1 teaspoon pepper

After the bird has been removed from the roasting pan, take out the rack and place pan on top of the stove. Dissolve the red currant jelly in the hot cooking fluids; add the seasoning and the flour. Cook until thickened.

Barbecued Ducklings

2 ducklings	1 teaspoon Worcestershire sauce
¼ cup lemon juice	1 garlic clove, crushed
¼ cup butter	1 tablespoon paprika
2 tablespoons onions, finely chopped	1 teaspoon salt
	¼ teaspoon pepper

Clean and skin the ducklings and wash them thoroughly. Cut into serving pieces and place in a greased baking dish. Put the butter in an 8-inch skillet and heat until it gives off a nutty aroma. Add the finely chopped onions and cook until golden brown. Add the lemon juice, Worcestershire sauce, garlic, paprika, salt, and pepper; simmer for 5 minutes. Remove from heat and pour over the ducklings.

Cover with aluminum foil and place in a 350°F oven for 1 hour or until tender, basting with the cooking fluids at frequent intervals. Serve as hot as possible with red currant jelly.

eeSanders

CHAPTER 10

The Staff of Life

When Columbus came to America, he found that a staple item in the diet of the Indians was a bread made from maize or corn. We do not know how long the North American Indians had been making bread, but we do know that the history of baking dates back to about 10,000 B.C.

Bread, man's first manufactured food, still remains his staff of life. Some scientists have estimated that man existed for 400,000 years by cultivating seeds for food before he augmented his diet with meat and fish. The early cereal grains used were rye, barley, millet, and wheat. Wheat can be grown on most of the earth's surface, except the polar and equatorial regions.

The discovery of fermentation necessitated a change in baking methods. Baking over coals as the Greeks did was given up, and ovens were constructed. These ovens, usually erected outdoors, can still be seen in use in the Province of Quebec and in New Mexico. The principle of the bake oven was that the hollow part of the oven was filled with firewood at night, the fire was lit, and burned all night. In the morning, the coals were raked out, the oven was swept, and the bread was baked on the floor of the oven. This method, or baking in a wood-burning stove, still produces better bread than bread baked in a gas or an electric oven.

BREAD MAKING

Flour

There is no accurate rule by which the grade of flour can be determined by examination and it is well that you stick to a brand that you are used to. Don't heed friends who urge you to change brands. What is liked by one can be a failure for another.

Good flour has a cream-white tint and should never look blue-white. Good flour should adhere to the hand when pressed down and show the imprint of the lines of the skin.

Flour should always be sifted before using. It is a good idea to sift it into a large pail or container with a tight-fitting lid so you do not have to sift it each time you use it.

Yeast

After the flour, yeast is the most essential element in bread baking. There are many varieties, such as hop-yeast, bakers' yeast, and dehydrated yeast. The problem usually is to convert the recipe from one form of yeast to another. Remember that one envelope dehydrated or dry yeast equals one cake compressed yeast or 3 tablespoons bakers' yeast.

The Sponge and Kneading

The whole secret of good bread lies in the making of the sponge and kneading. Today we have been spoiled with instant this or that but there is no such thing as an instant sponge. It takes time and hard labor to make a good sponge, and experience is the best teacher. Following are general instructions for bread making. While modern yeasts and super-refined flours do not require such long risings, or as much kneading, you will find these guidelines useful, and they will be essential if you plan to use coarse flours.

The sponge is made from warm water (or milk), yeast, and flour. I like to use water in which potatoes have been boiled because potato water keeps the bread moist longer. As a general rule, a pint of water or milk should be used for each quart of flour. (One quart equals 10 cups all-purpose flour.) The milk or water should be at blood heat temperature.

If using milk, scald it to prevent souring, but the bread will be coarse if the "wetting" is too hot. If only water is used, the addition of one tablespoon of butter or lard will make the bread more tender. Bread made with water will keep longer and will have the true flavor of the wheat more than if made with milk. When the sponge is made from milk alone, it requires more flour and longer kneading. When mixing the sponge in summer, it should never be set before 9 or 10 o'clock in the evening — when it is cooler.

When setting the sponge, test the milk or heated water with your finger. Have it as hot as your finger will take without burning. When the flour is added it will cool enough to take the yeast without spoiling the bacteria in the yeast. Cover the sponge with a baking blanket and set aside in a warm place (80 to 90°F) overnight. Ideally the sponge should be placed in a draft-free place inside a crock or stone jar which you have pre-heated.

The next morning put the sponge in a large dish with a tight-fitting cover. Put the required amount of flour into it and add 2 teaspoons of salt and mix well, making sure that the sponge is not too stiff. Turn out on the breadboard and knead without stopping until the dough no longer sticks to your hands or the board.

All the flour used for a recipe should be put in at this time. This first kneading of the dough is the most important and will take the most time. There are many different ways to knead — use the method that is most comfortable for you. When through with the kneading, form a large loaf, sprinkle the bread pan with a little flour, and place the dough in the pan, sprinkling a little flour on top to prevent the baking blanket which must cover it, from sticking to the dough. Cover tightly and let rise for 2 to 3 hours, or until the dough has doubled in size. Remove the cover and push the dough down. (Very little kneading is needed at this time.) Form into loaves in well-greased baking pans; grease the tops with salted butter; place in a warm spot and cover well with the blanket again. When it has again doubled in size, the dough is ready for the oven.

Baking

A moderate, uniformly heated oven is necessary for baking bread. A good, old-fashioned way to find out if the oven is hot enough is to stick your hand and arm into the oven; if it cannot be held there longer than you can count to twenty at a moderate tempo it is the right temperature. Or, you can test it by placing a small quantity of flour on a piece of old crockery in the centre of the oven; if it browns in one minute the heat is right.

To find out when the bread is done, test with a small broom straw. If nothing adheres to the straw when it is withdrawn, the bread is baked. As a general rule, it takes from 45 minutes to 1 hour to bake a loaf. As soon as the bread has been removed from the oven, the loaves should be taken from the pans and the entire outside should be greased with melted butter. Tilt the loaves on edge on a clean cloth on a bread rack, cover with the bread blanket, and let cool slowly.

BREAD RECIPES

Hardtack or Flatbread

Hardtack or flatbread was favored by the early settlers and scouts because it was easy to carry on long trips in the wilderness, being almost weightless. It would not go stale for months on end. Also, the whole rye was nourishing. It was used as a substitute for soft bread, or, it could be softened in water and boiled to make a palatable porridge when mixed with wild berries. Served with milk, this was an easy dish to prepare in the wilderness. Another method was to crumble it in a bowl, add a handful of cranberries, a little sugar, and milk.

Rye Hardtack

This recipe comes from a 150-year-old handwritten cookbook. It tastes good, is nourishing, and is light for the traveler to carry.

2 cups graham flour	1 cup lard, melted
2 teaspoons salt	2 cups buttermilk
1 teaspoon baking soda	white flour

In a large mixing bowl, blend the graham flour, salt, and soda. Add the boiling hot lard and stir well. Add the buttermilk (which should be at room temperature).

Knead in enough flour to make the dough hard enough to roll paper thin. Place on top of the stove to cook, or use a heavy pancake grill. Each piece should be a 10-inch circle with a centre hole.

The bread will bake in a very short time. Remove it from the stove and hang it on long rods in the pantry to dry.

Quick Brown Bread

2 cups all-bran	1 cup brown sugar
2 cups sour milk	1 cup raisins, softened in ½ cup
2 cups white flour	boiling water
2 teaspoons soda	1 teaspoon shortening
2 teaspoons molasses	1 teaspoon salt
2 envelopes of yeast	

Put all the ingredients in a bowl and mix thoroughly. Grease 4 bread forms and fill ⅔ full with the dough. Bake at 325°F for 45 minutes.

Rye Bread

2 cups water	1 tablespoon lard
¼ cup brown sugar	2 yeast cakes
¼ cup honey	4 cups white flour
1½ teaspoons caraway seed	1 teaspoon salt
1 teaspoon anise seed	2 cups rye flour

Heat together water, sugar, honey, spices, and lard; cool to luke-warm. Add yeast, mix well, and add about 3 cups of white flour. Beat thoroughly. Add rye flour, salt, and more white flour. Make a dough that can be handled easily, turn out on floured board and knead until satiny and elastic. Place dough in a greased bowl, cover, and let rise until doubled, about 2 to 4 hours. Knead and shape into loaves, place in bread pans, brush top with melted shortening, and let rise again for 1 to 2 hours. Bake in a 350°F oven about 1 hour.

Swedish Rye Bread

1 package yeast	1/3 cup shortening
½ cup warm water	2 teaspoons salt
2 cups boiling water	1 tablespoon caraway seed
2 cups rye flour	6 cups white flour
¾ cup molasses	

Dissolve yeast in warm water. Mix sifted rye flour, molasses, short-ening, salt, and caraway seed. Pour the boiling water over. Cool. Stir in yeast mixture. Add the white flour, enough to make a stiff dough. Knead well, cover, and set aside in a warm place to rise until doubled in size. Knead down and let rise again. Divide into 3 parts. Let rise for 15 minutes. Shape into 3 round loaves and place on cookie sheet. Let rise until double in size. Bake at 350°F for 40 minutes.

French Bread

Put 1 cup warm water in a bowl and add:

1 package yeast	2 tablespoons shortening
1 teaspoon salt	3¾ cups white flour
2 tablespoons sugar	

Mix well; turn out on a lightly floured board and knead until elastic (about 8 to 10 minutes). Place in a greased bowl, brush top with melted shortening, cover, and let rise until doubled in bulk. Punch down and let rise again. Punch down, and form a long narrow loaf, rolling it gently back and forth to lengthen loaf and to taper ends. Place on a lightly greased cookie sheet; sprinkle with corn meal. Make slashes at 2-inch intervals, brush with cold water, and let rise (uncovered). Brush again with cold water and sprinkle with sesame seeds. Bake at 375°F for 30 minutes.

White Bread

2 packages dry yeast, dissolved in ½ cup warm water
3½ cups warm liquid (milk, water, potato water, or half milk, half water)
¼ cup sugar
2 tablespoons salt
¼ cup shortening
11-12 cups sifted white flour

Stir sugar, salt, and shortening into liquid, then beat in 4 cups flour and the yeast with a rotary beater or spoon until smooth. Add remaining flour until the dough leaves sides of bowl. Turn out on lightly floured board and knead until dough becomes smooth and elastic and not sticky — about 15 minutes. Place in a large, greased bowl. Grease top of dough, cover with waxed paper, and baking blanket; let rise in a warm place, 80-90°F until doubled in bulk (1 to 2 hours).

Punch down in bowl and let rise again. Divide dough into 4 parts, and round each portion. Let rise for 15 minutes. Shape into 4 loaves; place in 9 x 5 x 3 inch baking pans; let rise in a warm place until dough reaches top of pan and fills corners (1½ to 2 hours). Bake in 375°F. oven for one hour.

Whole Wheat Bread

2½ cups finely mashed potatoes
½ cup sugar
7 cups potato water
3 cups warm water
1 tablespoon salt
2 packages yeast
5 cups whole wheat flour
8 cups white flour
1 cup lard, melted

In the evening boil enough potatoes to make 2½ cups of well-mashed potatoes. Save 7 cups potato water and add to it the mashed potatoes, ½ cup sugar, and 1 tablespoon salt. Add 2 packages yeast, stir well, and let rise overnight. In the morning, add 3 cups of warm water. Stiffen with 5 cups whole wheat flour and add the 8 cups of white flour and the melted lard. Work down twice, then mold into loaves; let rise in a warm spot. Bake in a 425° oven for 15 minutes, then lower the heat to 375°F for 45 minutes more.

SOURDOUGH

As North American settlers moved westward, the trailblazers, farmers, adventurers, and gold seekers had one thing in common — the sourdough starter. The legendary sourdough, whether at the back of the settler's kitchen stove, or carried on prospectors' backs, or in chuck wagon trains, was always in evidence.

I remember traveling with an Indian guide and his wife. During the day she carried the sourdough starter in a pouch made of doeskin hung with a string around her neck; at night she slept with it in her blanket roll. Consequently we had fresh sourdough bread almost every night. In the pioneer days of the American west, wherever there was a human being there was also, almost invariably, a pot of sourdough. Nowadays, with fresh and dehydrated yeast readily available, the need for sourdough starter has diminished to the point that its use has almost vanished.

Sourdough, according to Webster's dictionary, is "leaven, especially fermented dough, saved from baking so that it can be used in the next, thus avoiding the need for fresh yeast." The best way to get some sourdough starter is to find someone who has a well-established sourdough. Our sourdough starter is over one-hundred years old and is still going strong. It was a gift from Sourdough Jack in California and originated on the Kenai Peninsula of Alaska. A little sourdough will go a long way and will last for many years if properly taken care of.

If you cannot get hold of any, make your own: In the evening boil enough potatoes to make one pint when finely mashed. Save the potato water and add more water to it to make 3 pints. Add 1 tablespoon salt, ½ cup sugar, and 1 cake of compressed yeast to the potato water. Combine with the potatoes and stir well. Cover and let rise overnight. The next morning save one pint for your next baking.

For anyone who might have access to old bread recipes, here is another recipe for sourdough starter.

2 cups flour	1 package dry, granulated yeast
2 cups warm water	1 yeast cake

In a bowl, mix the ingredients well and put the bowl in a warm place or, in the oven overnight with the heat on as low as possible. The next morning, the dough should be bubbly and frothy. Some people call this the sponge or spoke yeast. Take out a cup of starter, put it in a scalded (to sterilize) pint sealer with a tight cover and store in the refrigerator for future baking. Then proceed with your recipe.

CARE AND USE OF SOURDOUGH STARTER

First of all, each time you set a sponge, remember to remove a cupful of it (before anything is added) and put it back into your sourdough pot. Keep your starter in an earthenware crock with a tight-fitting lid. If you do not use the starter every day, store the crock in the refrigerator; it will keep forever.

Sourdough starter raises bread much more slowly than yeast, so remember to set the starter the night before you intend to bake bread or pancakes. Here is how to use sourdough starter: Place the starter from your pot in a stainless-steel or glass container; add 2 cups of warm water (up to 90°F) and 2½ cups of flour. Mix thoroughly. The mixture will be thick and lumpy but the fermentation will thin it down and it will be lively in the morning. Cover bowl and let the dough sit in a warm spot overnight. Remember, today's kitchens are much cooler than in the old days when the woodstove was kept going all night.

Important: In the morning take 1 cup of the basic batter and put it in your sourdough pot.

SOURDOUGH RECIPES

Sourdough Pinch-offs

This is a quick bread. Traditionally, the dough was pinched off and baked in a Dutch oven.

½ cup sourdough starter	2 tablespoons honey
1 cup milk	¾ teaspoon salt
2½ cups whole wheat flour	1 teaspoon baking powder
½ teaspoon baking soda	bacon fat

Mix the starter, milk, and one cup of the flour in a large bowl. Let stand overnight in a warm place to rise. In the morning, turn this very soft dough out on one cup of flour on a board. Melt the honey in a little warm water and add to the dough. Combine the soda, salt, and baking powder with the remaining ½ cup of flour. Sprinkle it over the dough (on the baking board). Work the dry ingredients into the dough with your hands, kneading lightly. Roll out to ½-inch thickness. Cut out the biscuits with a cutter and dip each in bacon fat. Place either in a Dutch oven or close together in a square pan and set in a warm place to rise for about half an hour.

Bake in a moderately hot oven (375°F) for about 30 minutes.

136

Sourdough Blueberry Muffins

Put the starter in a bowl; add 2 cups of warm water and 2½ cups of flour. Mix well. Set in a warm place overnight. Remove one cup of the dough and put it back in the starter pot.

remaining sourdough	1 teaspoon baking soda
1½ cups whole wheat flour	½ cup melted bacon grease
½ cup sugar	2 eggs
1 teaspoon salt	2 cups fresh blueberries
½ cup evaporated milk	

Mix the flour, sugar, salt, and soda in a bowl. Mix eggs, bacon fat, and milk, and add to the remaining sourdough. Mix well. Add dry ingredients and mix thoroughly. Then add the fresh blueberries.

When in the bush make individual muffin tins out of aluminum foil formed over a round piece of wood. Grease the tins and fill about three-quarters full. Bake in a mud oven for about 30 to 35 minutes. If you do not have a mud oven, a reflector oven made from a tin can will do.

Sourdough Golden Honey Bread

This recipe was given to me by an old sourdough in Alaska. I have never tasted bread so light and golden. Put the starter in a bowl, add two cups warm water, and two cups whole wheat flour. Let stand overnight in a warm place. Take away one cup of the dough and put it back in the sourdough pot. To the remainder of the dough add:

4 cups whole wheat flour	2 teaspoons salt
2 cups milk	2 teaspoons baking soda
2 tablespoons butter or bacon fat	½ cup wild honey
¼ cup sugar	

Scald the milk and melt the fat and honey in it. Cool to lukewarm. Mix the sugar, salt, and soda. Blend together the basic dough, the milk mixture, and two cups of flour. Sprinkle the sugar, salt, and soda mixture on top of the dough and stir gently. Set dough in a warm place, covered with a cloth, for 30 minutes. Sift in the remaining two cups of flour until the dough is too stiff to stir with a spoon.

Turn out on a floured board and start to knead, adding enough wheat flour to keep the dough smooth and firm. Knead until light and satiny. Divide into sections or flatten it out into round cakes. Grease the tops and set in a warm spot. Let it double in bulk.

Bake in a moderate 325°F oven until it sounds hollow when thumped on top, about one hour. Remove from the oven and turn out on a floured towel. Butter the top crusts.

Sourdough Rye Bread

To the sourdough starter add 2 cups whole wheat flour and 2½ cups of warm water. Let it stand overnight in a warm, draft-free place. The next morning, use all the sourdough, except the cup that goes back into the sourdough pot.

basic sourdough starter	1 teaspoon anise seeds
¼ cup brown sugar	1 tablespoon bacon fat
¼ cup honey	1 teaspoon salt
1½ teaspoons caraway seeds	2 cups rye flour

Heat together in a little water, the sugar, honey, spices, and bacon fat. Cool to lukewarm. Add the mixture to the sourdough and beat well, adding the rye flour during the beating.

Turn out on a floured board and knead until the dough is smooth and satiny. Put it in a greased bowl, cover with waxed paper and a towel. Let rise until doubled in size, about 2 to 4 hours.

Knead and shape into loaves or round cakes. Place on cookie sheets; brush with melted shortening or sugar water. Keep in a warm, draft-free place and let rise until doubled. Bake in a moderate oven 375°F for an hour.

Fresh Fruit Breakfast Rolls

¾ cup sourdough starter	½ teaspoon baking soda
1 cup evaporated milk	1½ teaspoon salt
4 cups whole wheat flour	4 tablespoons bacon fat
½ cup honey	¼ cup brown sugar
1 egg	1 teaspoon cinnamon
1 teaspoon baking powder	1 cup blueberries

Mix starter, milk and two cups of the flour in a bowl. Cover and let stand at the back of the stove or in a warm place overnight. The next morning, melt the honey and bacon fat; cool, then mix in the egg and beat until frothy. Add this to the sourdough. Sift together the remaining flour, soda, baking powder, and salt. Sprinkle over the dough and mix thoroughly.

Turn out on a floured bread board and knead until smooth and velvety. Add just enough to keep the dough from sticking to the board.

Roll dough into a rectangle, approximately 16 by 8 inches. Mix the brown sugar and cinnamon and sprinkle over the dough. Spread the blueberries evenly over the top and roll (like a jelly roll), starting from the long side of the dough. Cut into 9 rolls.

Brush the bottoms and tops with a little melted butter and place in a square pan. Cover the pan with a towel and let rise in a warm place until doubled in size. Bake in a medium oven (375°F) for about 35 to 40 minutes.

Sourdough Corn Bannock

This recipe was given to me by an old trapper one cold morning on the trail while we were in the Rockies hunting grizzly bear. "If the grizzly don't come to taste this bannock, he is gone for good," said the old man as he walked over to his bedroll to get his sourdough starter.

1½ cups yellow cornmeal, uncooked	3 tablespoons sugar
1¾ cups evaporated milk, diluted	1 cup sourdough starter
	¼ cup bacon fat
2 eggs	¾ teaspoon salt
	¼ teaspoon soda

Combine cornmeal and milk in a bowl. Add the eggs, sugar, and starter and beat thoroughly. Add the melted bacon fat, salt, and soda, stirring until blended. Place your frying pan in the fire and melt some fat to grease the pan. Spoon the dough into the frying pan. Put the pan over the fire and cook for 5 minutes. Then, prop the pan vertically in front of the fire and bake until done, about 15 to 20 minutes or until a wood sliver inserted in the middle comes out clean.

Sourdough Pancakes

remaining dough (after starter has been removed)	½ cup evaporated milk
1 egg	1 teaspoon salt
2 tablespoons oil or melted lard	1 teaspoon baking soda
	2 tablespoons sugar

Place the dough in a bowl and add egg, oil, and milk. Mix well. Combine salt, soda, and sugar; sprinkle over the dough and mix. This will leaven and cause a foaming action. Let mixture rest for about 5 minutes. Heat a griddle and grease it well.

Drop the batter by tablespoonfuls on the hot griddle. (Sourdough pancakes require a hotter griddle than ordinary pancakes.) Flip over. If the batter does not drop off the spoon smoothly, it means it was not warm enough during the night for proper fermentation. Add a little milk to the dough to get the right consistency. Serves 4.

Sourdough Oatmeal Cookies

When traveling in the north, one is often surprised by the variety of delicious cookies and cakes made from sourdough starter. City people who have never had the experience of eating these delights, doubt that the sour-smelling starter can produce such sweet-tasting cookies and cakes. Try this recipe and you will be convinced!

1½ cups domestic or wild honey	½ teaspoon cloves
1 cup shortening or bacon fat	2 teaspoons spicebush powder
2 cups thick sourdough starter	1 teaspoon baking soda
3 cups rolled oats	2 cups whole wheat flour
1 teaspoon cinnamon	

Mix honey and shortening well. Add the sourdough and rolled oats. Combine remaining ingredients, sprinkle on top of the batter, and mix well with your fingers. Refrigerate for an hour. Roll out the dough on a floured board and cut with a cookie cutter. Place cookies on a greased cookie sheet and bake for about 15 minutes in a moderate oven, 375°F. Cool and serve, or, if you want to make a double cookie, use cooked dates or strawberry jam as a filling.

Sourdough Doughnuts

This recipe was given to me by Mrs. Oscar Berg who lives in a small Norwegian settlement in northwestern Ontario. She claims that by using this method for making doughnuts, you cannot go wrong. We have to agree, as we have never had it fail.

2 cups white flour	1 egg
1 teaspoon baking powder	½ cup sugar
½ teaspoon salt	1 cup sourdough starter
½ teaspoon baking soda	½ cup milk
1 teaspoon cinnamon	2 teaspoons oil

Sift the first five ingredients together. Beat together the egg and sugar; stir in the sourdough, then add the milk and oil. Add the sifted ingredients to the dough. Knead on a floured board into a fairly stiff dough. Roll it out to ½-inch thickness and cut out doughnut shapes with a cookie cutter.

Place the doughnuts on a greased cookie sheet. Cover and let rise in a warm oven for 1 hour. With a spatula, lift them carefully off the sheet and drop into deep fat heated to about 370°F. Fry to a rich golden brown. Drain on absorbent paper. Roll in a mixture of sugar and cinnamon, if desired.

Sourdough Chocolate Cake

Sitting in Trapper Sven's cabin watching the big Swede, whose hands are the size of dinner plates, no one would think he could handle as delicate an instrument as an egg beater without crushing it into a mass of bent wires and broken gears. But when he makes a cake, he is as precise as a surgeon. After tasting this masterpiece we wondered why this man was living in the wilderness when he could have been a chef in a four-star restaurant. Here is the recipe he gave us.

½ cup sourdough starter	½ teaspoon salt
1 cup water	1 teaspoon vanilla
1½ cups flour	1 teaspoon cinnamon
½ cup evaporated milk	2 teaspoons baking soda
1 cup sugar	2 eggs
½ cup shortening	3 squares semi-sweet chocolate

In a bowl, combine the sourdough starter with the water, flour, and milk. Mix well and place in a warm spot for about 3 hours.

Cream the sugar, shortening, salt, vanilla, cinnamon, and baking soda. Add the eggs, one at a time, and beat well. Combine the creamed mixture and the melted chocolate with the sourdough; fold together, making sure all is well blended.

Pour the batter into one 9-inch-square pan and bake at 350°F for about 30 minutes. Remove from oven and cool upside down on a plate.

CHAPTER 11

Simple Fare

HOW TO MAKE CHEESE

Making cheese is a relatively simple art, and a lot of fun besides. Goat's milk, cow's milk, and ewe's milk are most commonly used, although making cheese from camel, donkey, and reindeer milk is common practice in some parts of the world.

Pasteurization

To produce a superior product, always start with fresh, raw milk. Many people do not like to use raw milk, so if you do not have an electric pasteurizer, improvise with a large double boiler and follow this method of pasteurization:

Heat water in the bottom of a double boiler until the milk in the top boiler reaches a temperature of 145°F. Keep milk at this temperature for 30 minutes. (You might have to adjust the heat several times to maintain an even temperature of 145°F.)

Cool the milk to 72°F. You can do this simply by emptying the hot water in the bottom pan and replacing it with cool water.

If you are making cottage cheese, proceed with the milk at this temperature. If you intend to store the milk for later use, cool it to 50°F and store in refrigerator or spring house.

Curds and Whey Rennet, an indispensable ingredient in cheesemaking, is an animal product made from the stomach acid of young calves. When added to milk, it causes liquid to separate from the solids. The liquid is whey, the solid the curd. If the milk is sweet and cold, the curds are harder. I remember as a boy on the farm we used extracts from the wild thistle and the wild artichoke, which also coagulate milk. (We also used the juice from marigold petals to add a golden color to our cheese or butter.) After the curd has separated, the cheese must be drained, the drainage process depending on the cheese you are making.

Some cheeses are salted and eaten right away, such as Italian ricotta. Others are cut, kneaded, cooked, pressed, ground, and pressed again. This process is called cheddaring. After draining, the cheese may be ripened, but how this final stage is done and for how long varies greatly from cheese to cheese. Blue cheese, which was originally made from ewe's milk, is inoculated with mold, and, within a few months, the characteristic green veins find their way deep into the cheese. Banon, a French cheese made from goat's milk, is cured in chestnut leaves, dried, and then passed through the dregs of wine casks, and fermented in stone crocks. Press ost, a hard Swedish cheese, is washed in whiskey for five months during the curing.

There are thousands of different cheeses in the world, each depending on its native soil, each unique, as cheese is one of the most ancient foods manufactured by man. We consider it to be a gift of the land, a measure of the slow rhythm of country life.

Cottage Cheese

The first step is to make the clabber. This is milk which has been allowed to sour at room temperature. The souring process can take as long as a week during the winter, and as little as a day in the heat of the summer. Use unpasteurized skim milk or buttermilk only, because pasteurized milk does not sour properly.

The clabber is ready when it is of a jelly-like consistency. Crosshatch the clabber with a knife. (Cream cheese can be made at this stage by hanging the clabber overnight in a cheesecloth bag. This separates the curds and whey.)

Once crosshatched, gently heat the clabber in a double boiler, stirring it occasionally. The water should be too hot to touch but never boiling; the clabber, however, should never get too hot to touch. When the clabber has shrunk uniformly into small pieces, it is done. Personal experience is the best way to get it right. Strain the mixture through a colander. If the curds run through the holes in the colander, it is underdone; if they are dry and rubbery, it is overdone. Add a little salt and cream to taste.

(From *The People's Home Library 1848.*)

144

Basic Recipe for Hard Cheese

(Eight quarts of milk render 1½ to 2 pounds of cheese)

8 quarts fresh, whole milk   **2 tablespoons salt**
¼ of a rennet tablet

Preparation of milk   Allow 4 quarts of the evening's milk to ripen overnight in a cool place (50-60°F.) Mix in 4 quarts of the next morning's milk. This will give a better cheese than if you use all fresh milk; the milk, however, must taste sweet. Either cow's or goat's milk can be used with equally good results.

Warming the milk   Heat the milk to 86°F in an enamel or tin pail.

Add cheese rennet   Dissolve ¼ of a cheese rennet tablet in a glass of cold water. To help dissolve it, break and crush it with a spoon in the water; stir until completely dissolved. Put the pail of milk in a larger pail of warm water (88-90°F.) Leave it in a warm place, protected from drafts. Add the rennet solution and stir milk thoroughly for a minute after rennet is added.

Let stand 30-45 minutes   Let stand undisturbed until a firm curd forms. Test the firmness of curd with your finger; put finger into the curd at 45° angle and lift. If the curd breaks clean over your finger, it is ready to cut.

Cutting the curd   To cut the curd into small cubes, use a long butcher knife, long enough so the blade will go to the bottom of the pail without touching the surface with the handle. Insert the knife blade through the curd right to the bottom of the container on the opposite side. Then pull the knife, held vertically, toward you. Withdraw the knife and repeat every ⅜ inch. Turn the container a quarter turn, repeat the first step, again cutting the curd every ⅜ inch.

     Turn the container to its original cut line and cut at an angle, starting about 1 inch from the side of the pail, slicing the curd into pieces about ½ to 1-inch thick, beginning at the top, and making each subsequent cut about ½ to 1 inch lower. Then, turn the pail and make similar angular cuts from the other side.

Stir curd by hand   With your hand, stir curd thoroughly but very gently, with long, slow movements, taking care not to squash the curd. Try to make the pieces as nearly the same size as possible. Stir continuously by hand for 15 minutes, to prevent the curd from sticking together.

Heat the curd slowly Heat slowly to 102°F, raising the temperature of the curds and whey about 1½ degrees every 5 minutes. Stir with a spoon often enough to keep the curd from sticking together. Heating should continue slowly and, if necessary, to a few degrees above 102°F, until the curd holds its shape but falls apart easily when held for a few seconds without squeezing.

Stop heating, stir Remove from heat. Stir every 5-10 minutes or often enough to keep curd from matting together. Leave curd in the warm whey until it becomes firm enough that when a handful of the pieces are pressed together they shake apart easily. This will take about an hour.

Pour curd into cheesecloth Drape a cheesecloth (3 to 4 square feet) over a pail fastening it to the sides with a pair of clothespins. Pour the cheese into the cheesecloth. Then, holding two corners of the cloth in each hand, let the curd roll back and forth (without sticking together), for about 2 or 3 minutes to allow the whey to run off.

Salt the curd Place cloth with curd in an empty pail; sprinkle 1 tablespoon salt over the curd; mix well with hands without squeezing, then sprinkle another tablespoon of salt on the curd and mix well again.

Form into a ball and hang it Tie the four corners of the cheesecloth crosswise, forming the curd into a ball. Hang for ½ to ¾ hour to drain.

Dress the cheese Remove the cheesecloth. Fold a long cloth, shaped like a dish towel, into a bandage about 3 inches wide and wrap it tightly around the ball, forming it into a round shape. Pin it in place. With your hands, press the cheese down to make the top surface smooth. There should be no cracks extending into the centre of the cheese. The round loaf of cheese should not be more than six inches across; otherwise it will dry out too much.

Press the cheese Place three or four thicknesses of cheesecloth on top and under the cheese. Put the cheese on the lower board of the cheese press. Tighten down press moderately. In the evening, turn the cheese and increase the pressure. Let stand until morning.

Paraffin and store Remove cloths and place cheese on a board for a day, turning it occasionally until the rind is completely dry. Then dip it in paraffin that has been heated (210° to 220°F) in a double boiler. Dip first one side, wait a minute, then dip the other side. (Remove the paraffin pot from the source of heat while you are doing the dipping, as even one drop spilled on the stove may catch fire and then the whole thing will burst into flames.)

146

Store the cheese in a clean, cool, but frost-free cellar or similar place. Turn it over every day for a few days, then 2 or 3 times a week. The cheese is usually good to eat after 4 to 5 weeks, but if you can wait for a year or two, it is even better.

Blue Cheese Culture

Take a mold culture from aged blue cheese and put it on a loaf of bread. Keep in a moist, dark place or, even better, wrap in cheesecloth and let stand for 6 weeks. When the bread has completely crumbled and the mold has separated, crush the mold into a powder. Bottle and cork tightly.

To use: Sprinkle dried mold on the cheese, or, pierce it into the cheese with the head of a needle in several places. Salt lightly and let rest for several days. When the mold has had a good start, pierce the cheese at least 60 times to air the mold deep in the interior. Keep in a cool, dark place. Age 2 to 5 months.

Neufchatel Cheese

This cheese is made from whole goat's milk. It is a soft cheese suitable for spreading on bread. I like it lightly pressed so that I can slice it and put it on sourdough bread.

1 gallon sweet goat's milk   **1 tablespoon salt**
1 junket tablet

Put one gallon of sweet, whole goat's milk in a double boiler. Heat the milk to 72°F. (Use a dairy or candy thermometer.) Add one junket tablet dissolved in ½ cup of cold water, and stir thoroughly.

The warm milk should sit overnight (12 to 15 hours). In the morning, the curd will be firm and smooth, with a little whey on top. Spread a clean cheesecloth over a colander and ladle the curd into it. Tie the ends of the cloth together and hang the ball up to drain. Do not throw the whey away; drink it or feed it to the livestock. It is too valuable to waste, since it contains milk sugar (lactose), minerals, and albumen. In Sweden a cheese called Mysost is made out of goat's milk whey.

As the cheese drips, the curds can be stirred occasionally. The more whey removed, the milder the flavor. If you want an extra mild cheese, run cold water over the curds. After draining, add salt to taste. It is now ready to eat or, you can put it in a cheese press overnight for a slightly harder cheese.

CHEESE RECIPES

One of the most delightful dining customs is to serve cheese with fruit for dessert. In our family we do not only use homemade cheese as a dessert; we have adopted some of the early French settlers' customs and use cheese in many dishes; from a slice of buttered bread, covered with cheese and a couple strips of bacon and broiled under the grill for a few minutes, to elaborate soups and cheesecakes. Here are some of our most cherished recipes:

Cheese and Ham Dip

2 cups grated old cheese	¼ cup chopped green onion
2 cups ham, finely chopped	½ teaspoon dry mustard
¾ cup mayonnaise (homemade)	¼ teaspoon pepper

Combine all ingredients; place in refrigerator until needed. Can be used as a dip, or as a spread on crackers, topped with an olive.

Quick Cheese Sauce

2 cups grated old cheese	¼ teaspoon pepper
2/3 cup milk	¼ teaspoon paprika
¼ teaspoon salt	½ teaspoon dry mustard

Combine all ingredients and heat slowly in top of a double boiler over low heat, stirring until smooth. Serve with new potatoes, cauliflower, eggs, or ham.

Thick Cheese Sauce

¼ cup butter	¼ teaspoon paprika
¼ cup flour	½ teaspoon dry mustard
½ teaspoon salt	2 cups milk
¼ teaspoon pepper	2 cups grated old cheese

Melt butter in a double boiler, blend in flour and seasoning, gradually add milk. Cook over medium heat until mixture thickens, stirring constantly. Add the cheese. Beat well. Serve as hot as possible over vegetables, hard-boiled eggs, or fish.

148

Cheese Soup

1 cup chopped onion	¼ teaspoon pepper
½ cup diced celery	½ teaspoon salt
3 tablespoons butter	2 cups milk
1 tablespoon flour	2 cups grated old cheese
1 teaspoon dry mustard	4 slices bacon, fried and crumbled
¼ teaspoon paprika	

Melt the butter in a 7-inch frying pan. Add the onion and celery and sauté until onion is transparent (5-6 minutes). Blend in flour and seasonings. Gradually add milk and cook over medium heat until smooth and slightly thickened, stirring constantly. Add cheese and stir until melted. Serve immediately, garnished with crumbled bacon and finely chopped green onion. Serves 4.

Hamburg and Neufchatel Cheese Pie

1 cup finely chopped onion	1 teaspoon Worcestershire sauce
¼ cup finely chopped green pepper	2 tablespoons flour
2 tablespoons butter	1 9-inch pie shell, baked
1 pound minced beef	2 beaten eggs
¾ teaspoon salt	1 cup Neufchatel cheese
¼ teaspoon pepper	dash of paprika

Melt the butter in a frying pan until it gives off a nutty aroma; add the onion and green pepper and sauté until onion is transparent. Add meat and brown for 5 to 6 minutes. Stir in seasonings and flour. Spread on the bottom of the baked 9-inch pie shell.

Combine eggs and Neufchatel cheese, pour over meat mixture, and sprinkle with paprika. Bake at 350°F until browned, about 40 to 45 minutes. Serves 6.

Cheese Muffins

2 cups sifted all-purpose flour	1 egg, beaten
3 teaspoons baking powder	1 cup milk
½ teaspoon salt	¼ cup butter, melted
2/3 cup grated hard cheese	

Sift flour, baking powder, and salt. Stir in cheese. Combine egg, milk, and melted butter; stir quickly into flour mixture until mixed but still lumpy. Fill well-greased muffin tins two-thirds full. Bake at 400°F until golden brown, 20-25 minutes. Serve with bearberry jelly.

Cheese Apple Pie

5 cups sliced tart apples	¼ teaspoon cinnamon
3 tablespoons melted butter	1 9-inch pie shell, unbaked
½ cup sugar	4 slices old, hard cheese
1 tablespoon cornstarch	

Melt the butter and roll the apples in it until well coated. Mix sugar, cornstarch, and cinnamon. Sprinkle 2 tablespoons of this mixture over the surface of the pie shell. Combine the rest with the apples. Arrange apples in pie shell and cover with slices of cheese.

Topping

½ cup sifted flour	¼ teaspoon cinnamon
¼ cup brown sugar	¼ cup butter

Combine flour, brown sugar, and cinnamon. Cut in butter until mixture resembles coarse bread crumbs. Sprinkle over pie. Bake 15 minutes at 450°F. Reduce oven temperature to 350°F and continue baking until apples are tender, about 30 minutes more. Serves 6.

Baked Cheesecake

Crust

1½ cups crushed graham wafers	¼ cup butter, softened
2 tablespoons sugar	

Combine ingredients and press firmly on bottom and sides of greased 9-inch springform pan.

Filling

2 cups Neufchatel or cottage cheese	½ cup sifted all-purpose flour
1 pound cream cheese, softened	¼ teaspoon salt
¼ cup soft butter	4 eggs, separated
1 cup sugar	½ teaspoon lemon rind
	1 tablespoon lemon juice

Beat cottage cheese until smooth. Blend in cream cheese and butter. Add sifted dry ingredients. Fold in beaten egg yolks and add lemon rind and juice. Gently fold in stiffly beaten egg whites and pour into crumb crust. Bake 1 hour at 325°F. Turn off heat and leave cheesecake in oven 1 hour. Cool thoroughly before removing from pan.

3 cups canned pear halves	1/3 cup sugar
¾ cup pear juice	¼ teaspoon lemon rind
2 tablespoons cornstarch	¼ teaspoon lemon juice

Drain pears, reserving juice. Mix cornstarch and sugar, blend in pear juice and cook until thickened (about 15 minutes), stirring constantly. Stir in lemon rind and juice. Arrange pear halves on cheesecake and cover with glaze. Cool before cutting. Serves 8 to 12.

BUTTER

How well I remember as a boy on the farm, taking turns at the crank of the butter churn! Many hours each week were spent making butter, and even then I felt the result was well worth the hard work, as it was certainly not the speckled, spotted, and grizzled material that you buy in the stores today.

Can you think of anything more heavenly than the aroma of fresh bread lingering in a large country kitchen, and the bread, still warm from the oven, thickly spread with freshly churned butter? Why not try it?

If you have your own cows and a separator, use the cream (pasteurized) for making butter. Here is how it is done. Pour cream into a cream can and store it in a refrigerator or in a spring house for several days. (Cream kept cool for several days will churn much faster than fresh cream.) Now bring it to room temperature and let it ripen for at least 6 to 8 hours. It will thicken and sour slightly, eventually giving the butter a mild and wonderful flavor. Once the cream has ripened it should be cooled again before churning.

Pour the cooled cream into your homemade or store-bought butter churn; beat at high speed until flecks of butter begin to form and float to the surface. Then beat at low speed until the butter separates from the milk. As the butter forms, it will cling to the sides of the butter churn; keep pushing it down the sides with a wooden spoon or spatula. Pour off the buttermilk, measure the amount which is poured off, and replace it with the same amount of cool water. Still beating at low speed, continue pouring off water and replacing it with cool water until the butter clots and thickens.

Remove beaters and, with a wooden spoon, scrape the butter from them. Transfer the butter from the churn to a wooden bowl. With the help of two wooden spoons, squeeze out the water trapped in the butter by pressing the butter against the sides of the bowl. When all the water has been removed, add salt (if you like salted buttter). Sprinkle salt to taste over the butter; work it in thoroughly. Remove the butter from the bowl, put it in a butter press, and wrap with waxed paper or, even better, store the butter in a stone crock, sealing the top with wax. Keep in refrigerator or spring house. Homemade butter is very light in color.

YOGURT

One of the biggest problems the early settlers encountered was how to keep milk sweet without refrigeration. Failing this, yogurt was made as a substitute, and was often eaten as a dessert.

Yogurt is a cultured milk product made with *lactobacillus bulgaricus* and has been known to man since biblical times. It is wonderfully versatile — it can be made from cow, goat, buffalo, reindeer, mare, or ewe milk. In the pioneer days, yogurt culture was guarded as carefully as sourdough starter.

You can still make your own yogurt, but go to a health food store to buy the culture. Once you have the starter you can go on forever making your own.

1 quart whole pasteurized milk   1/3 ounce dry Bulgarian yogurt culture

In a 2-quart saucepan, heat the milk to 180°F. (A thermometer is useful but I have often made yogurt without one in the bush.) Cool the milk to about 100°F (lukewarm). Add the culture and mix well. Pour the mixture into small soup bowls or into one big bowl. Cover with clear plastic wrap and set in a warm place. I use a small wooden box in which I have installed a light socket with a 15-watt bulb. If I am in the bush, I place the milk in a quart jar and bury the bottle in the dying ashes of my campfire.

Whatever the method, it is vitally important that the mixture be left undisturbed for at least 5 hours, and sometimes for as long as 10 hours. When set, store in a cool place; a refrigerator if you are at home, a cold stream if on the trail.

Successive batches can be made by saving a small part of the yogurt (about 3 tablespoons for one quart) and using it as a starter for the next batch.

SAUSAGES

Sausages are an age-old farm staple. There are thousands of different types, each with its own racial or geographic origin. Sausages were traditionally made from scraps of meat, pork, and vegetables that in any other form could not be preserved. The modern-day homesteader must have a meat grinder equipped with a sausage filler to fill the casings quickly and efficiently. Sausage casings are usually made from animal intestines that have been scraped and cleaned. They can be bought from meat stores in a deep-salted form. Wash them in cold water, then blow through them to open.

Bologna

6 pounds ground beef	2 teaspoons ground allspice
4½ pounds ground pork	2 teaspoons salt
5 pounds potatoes	¼ cup onions, finely chopped

Boil the potatoes until peels slip off, then grind coarsely. Mix all the ingredients in a large mixing bowl. Put the mixture through the meat grinder into the casings. Fill the casings about half full. You will need 1½ pounds of casings.

Boil slowly until done (about 30 minutes). Store in a cold place.

Potato Sausage

2½ pounds round steak, ground	1½ quarts milk, cooked and
2½ pounds pork shoulder, ground	cooled
2½ pounds side pork, ground	2 tablespoons salt
3½ cups raw, peeled, and ground	2 teaspoons pepper
potatoes	½ teaspoon allspice

With your hands, knead all ingredients for half an hour. Equip your meat grinder with the casing filler, and fill the casings half full. Do not make the sausage too long. Store in freezer. When ready to use, remove from freezer and thaw in refrigerator. Boil for at least 30 minutes in lightly salted water.

Blood Sausage

2 quarts pork blood	1 tablespoon salt
½ teaspoon ginger	½ cup white flour
½ teaspoon allspice	½ cup rye flour
fresh pork, diced	

Fresh blood must be constantly stirred from the time it is taken from the pig (adding a little salt at the beginning), until combined with all ingredients except the diced pork. Stir until it starts to thicken. Make a loose paste and fill casings, adding diced pork as you go. Place in kettle

153

of salted water and boil for 1½ to 2 hours. Remove and cool. The sausages can be stored as they are, without freezing. To use, cut into slices and fry in bacon fat, sprinkling a little sugar on top of the slices as you fry them.

MEATS

While it is true that the better the meat the better the results, nevertheless good meat may be spoiled by poor cooking, whereas an inferior piece of meat can be made exceedingly palatable by knowing just how to cook it. Many appetizing dishes may be prepared from the so-called cheaper cuts of meat.

Never drop meat from your bill of fare as it is the main means of muscle building and repairing tissues in the body.

Skill in selecting meat is gained only through careful practice and a multitude of questions asked of those who know. Forget the nicely wrapped meat from the supermarket and get used to the different cuts that are used on the farm or homestead.

MEAT RECIPES

Roast Beef

To roast a piece of meat is no small art, and yet it is so easy to do it well. Remember that the oven should be very hot.

Wipe the meat with a wet or damp cloth; on top of the stove, heat to very hot an iron frying pan. Melt a tablespoon of butter in the frying pan and when the butter starts to brown, add one teaspoon of salt. Then sear the meat well on all sides. This will seal the juices and keep the meat moist during the cooking process. Place the roast in a roasting pan with a rack in the bottom. To the juices in the frying pan, add a cup of boiling water. Swish it around to loosen all the remains of the meat. Pour this over the roast in the roasting pan. Sprinkle about 1 teaspoon of pepper over the roast and put it in the oven. Baste often during the cooking period. Allow 20 minutes per pound roasting time. If you prefer well-done meat, increase the time to 30 minutes per pound.

Keep two things in mind. First, have the oven hot. Second, when the meat requires basting, baste it and let nothing interfere with this. Sometimes it pays to cover the top of the roast with a piece of double aluminum foil to prevent it from browning too much.

Pot Roast

3½ pounds beef shoulder	2 scraped carrots, cut into
¼ pound suet	pieces
1 large onion	2½ cups boiling water
1 tablespoon butter	salt
	pepper

Choose a thick cut of beef from the shoulder and wipe with a damp cloth. Have the kettle or dutch oven hot, put in the suet, and render the fat. During this time, heat an iron frying pan very hot, melt some butter in it, and sear the meat on all sides.

Remove the suet scraps from the fat, add the sliced onion, and cook until brown. Add the seared meat, carrots, and the water. Cover with a tight lid and simmer slowly 1 hour. Season with salt and pepper to taste and continue simmering until done, about 2 hours.

The secret of a good pot roast is more in the cooking than in the meat; never let it boil at any time.

Leave enough fluid in the kettle for gravy, which can be thickened with a tablespoon of flour after the meat has been removed.

Stuffed Onion Rolls

3 large onions (½ pound each)	2 tablespoons fresh bread crumbs
3 tablespoons butter	

Place the peeled onions in a 3-quart stainless steel saucepan, add enough water to cover, and bring to a boil over moderate heat. Lower the heat and simmer for 40 minutes uncovered.

Remove the onions from the pan with a slotted spoon, drain, and let cool on a platter while you make the meat stuffing.

Meat Stuffing

2 slices white bread	1 teaspoon salt
1 egg	½ teaspoon pepper
½ cup cream or milk	1 medium onion, grated
½ pound lean ground beef	

Remove the crusts from the bread and place the slices in a large mixing bowl. Add the egg and the milk or cream and let stand for 1 hour. Mix the bread, eggs, and milk well, making sure that the bread is well soaked and broken up; use a fork if necessary. Add the ground beef and the grated onions to the bread-egg mixture, sprinkle with salt and pepper, mix well with your hands, and set aside.

Pull off each onion layer separately. They should peel off quite easily. Use only the large outer layers. Discard the centre of the onion or use for some other purpose. Put a heaping tablespoon of the meat stuffing in the centre of each onion leaf. Enclose it by folding over the edges of the leaf.

Preheat the oven to 400°F. In a shallow 2-quart flameproof baking dish melt 3 tablespoons butter over low heat. Remove from the heat, roll the onion rolls in the butter and place them, sealed side down, side by side in the dish. Sprinkle with the bread crumbs and bake in the oven for 25 minutes, until the onions are lightly browned and the meat is cooked. You might have to cover the dish with aluminum foil to prevent too much browning.

Shepherd's Pie

2 pounds leftover roast beef	pepper
leftover gravy	5 medium potatoes
4 medium onions	1 tablespoon butter
salt	

Run the leftover meat and the raw onions through a meat mincer the night before the dish is to be eaten. Sprinkle with salt and pepper to taste, store in a cool place overnight. Peel, boil, and mash the potatoes.

Heat the gravy in a saucepan and set aside. Place the meat-onion mixture in a 2 quart fireproof oven dish to about 2 inches from the top. Stir in enough heated gravy to make the mixture moist. Spread the mashed potato on top of the meat, dot with butter, and bake in a 325°F oven for an hour. The top should be golden brown. Just before serving sprinkle the top with a little paprika.

Swedish Hash

5-6 medium potatoes, boiled and diced into ¼-inch pieces	2 tablespoons butter
1 pound roast of beef, diced into ¼-inch pieces	2 medium onions, finely chopped
½ pound smoked ham, diced into ¼-inch pieces	1 teaspoon salt
	½ teaspoon pepper
	4 fried eggs or 4 raw eggs

Melt the butter in a large iron frying pan. Add the onions and fry until golden yellow, then add the meat and stir well. Add the potatoes, cover the frying pan, and heat thoroughly, stirring occasionally.

Arrange individual servings on 4 warmed dinner plates, break a raw egg on top, and serve hot. If you prefer, fry the eggs sunny side up and place one on top of each serving.

Roulades of Beef Stuffed with Anchovies and Onions

2 pounds top round steak	1 cup onions, finely chopped
salt	2 tablespoons flour
1 teaspoon black pepper	16 flat anchovy fillets
4 tablespoons butter	½ cup water
4 tablespoons vegetable oil	

Cut the meat into 8 slices, 6 by 3 inches each. Pound them with the meat pounder until they are about ⅛ inch thick.

Heat 1 tablespoon of butter and 2 tablespoons of oil in a small skillet, add the onions, and fry until golden brown. Remove from heat and stir in the flour. Return to low heat and cook for 5 minutes. Remove 2 tablespoons of this roux for the sauce. Sprinkle each slice of meat with the pepper and salt. Spread the remainder of the roux evenly over the meat. Lay 2 anchovy fillets on each slice, roll them up tightly and secure with a toothpick inserted through the roll lengthwise.

Heat the remaining 3 tablespoons of butter and the 2 tablespoons of oil in a cast iron frying pan over moderate heat. When the foam subsides, add the meat rolls, four at a time. Turn the rolls over with kitchen tongs to brown them on all sides. Arrange the browned meat rolls in a single layer in a 2-quart casserole or baking dish with a lid.

Preheat the oven to 350°F. Deglaze the frying pan by pouring in ½ cup of water and let it come to a boil, scraping loose all bits and pieces of meat that have stuck to the bottom of the pan. Add the 2 tablespoons of reserved roux and cook over medium heat for 5 minutes, still stirring briskly, until the sauce has thickened. Pour over the meat rolls, cover, and bake in the oven for 45 minutes.

Smoked Bacon with Onions and Apple Rings

4 tablespoons butter	2 large onions, thinly sliced
1 pound bacon	1 teaspoon pepper
2 large tart cooking apples unpeeled, cored, and cut into ½-inch-thick rings	

Melt 2 tablespoons of the butter in a large skillet. When the butter gives off a nutty aroma, add the bacon. Fry for 10 minutes, or until the bacon is lightly browned. Remove from the skillet with a slotted spoon and set aside to drain on paper towels.

Fry the onion slices for 10 minutes in the fat remaining in the skillet, adding more butter if necessary. The onions should be golden brown and transparent. Add the apple rings and cover the skillet. Simmer over low heat for 15 minutes shaking the skillet occasionally to prevent the apples from sticking to the bottom. When the apples are tender, return the drained bacon to the skillet, simmer for an additional 10 minutes or until the bacon is heated through.

Sprinkle with pepper and serve directly from the skillet.

Coachman's Pan

2 pounds boiling potatoes	1½ cups beer
2 tablespoons butter	½ teaspoon sugar
2 tablespoons vegetable oil	1 teaspoon salt
3 medium onions, thinly sliced	½ teaspoon pepper
4 lamb kidneys, or 1 veal, or	1 bay leaf
2 pork kidneys	
¾ pound pork loin, cut into	
¼-inch slices	

Preheat the oven to 350°F. Peel potatoes and slice them ⅛-inch thick; set aside in a bowl with cold water and 2 drops of lemon juice to prevent discoloration.

Heat the butter and oil in a heavy 12-inch skillet over moderate heat. Add the onions and cook until golden brown. Remove from the skillet and set aside. Add more butter and oil to the skillet, and brown the kidneys and pork slices evenly but quickly, turning them with kitchen tongs several times. Remove the meat from the skillet and slice the kidneys into ¼-inch thick slices.

Deglaze the skillet by adding beer, beef stock, and sugar, scraping into the liquid any browned bits of onion or sediment clinging to the bottom and sides of the pan. Remove from heat and set aside.

Drain the potatoes and pat them dry with paper towels. Arrange 2 or 3 layers of potatoes, meat, and onions alternately in an oven-to-table casserole, finishing with layer of potatoes. Season each layer as you go with salt and pepper. Place the bay leaf in the centre of the top layer. Pour the liquid from the skillet on top. It should just cover the top layer in the dish. If it does not, add some more beef stock.

Bring the casserole to a boil on top of the stove, then cook in the oven for about 2 hours, or until the top layer of potatoes is brown and tender. Serve directly from the casserole with cranberry jelly.

CHAPTER 12

The Vegetable Garden

LOCATION, SOIL, AND FERTILIZER

Soon after you have settled in, start to look for a proper place for your vegetable garden. As for all growing crops, the most important factors for success are: soil fertility, good seed, the right tools, and careful preparation and cultivation of the land.

For convenient weeding, watering, and harvesting, the garden should be near the house. It should be in a sunny location, free from shade, and tree roots should not penetrate the area. Vegetables cannot compete with shade trees for food and moisture.

Deep, sandy loam containing sand, clay, and organic matter in a reasonable balance is the best. Gravelly loam and clay loam are also good. The greater the depth of the surface soil or top soil, the better the crops. Sandy loam and gravelly loam are easy to work and are classed as early soils because they warm up quickly in the spring. However, they lose moisture quickly during dry weather. Clay loam is more difficult to work and must be handled carefully. Digging or plowing this type of soil when wet or very dry causes lumpiness that makes the preparation of a fine seedbed difficult. Soil filled with tree roots is undesirable as these roots compete with the vegetables for plant food and moisture.

Do not be discuraged if you find that your piece of property does not have all the requirements for a good vegetable garden. A great many home or farm gardens are located on soils that are far from ideal, in which case the use of manure or compost becomes almost essential. If it can be obtained, well-rotted manure is an excellent soil conditioner. In addition to supplying plant food, it improves the structure of the soil. It makes sandy soil more suitable for plants, because the vegetable matter holds moisture more uniformly. Manure or compost materials open up clay soils so that air and water may penetrate better.

The plant food content of manures varies widely, depending on the type of animal from which it is produced and the animal's diet. Sheep and poultry manures are richer in plant food constituents than pig, horse, and cow manures. Pig manure is not often used but it may be excellent if the animals are getting a rich diet and plenty of litter. Because of its greater bulk and availability, cow manure is the most widely used on country vegetable gardens.

THE COMPOST PILE

Where manure is not readily available, artificial manure may be prepared by the decomposition of vegetable matter in compost piles. Humus-forming materials that might otherwise be wasted can be used in this way. Satisfactory materials for this purpose are hay, straw, peat, weeds, grass clippings, leaves, garden refuse that is not diseased, and even domestic garbage. In order to hasten decomposition, food should be supplied to the bacteria that bring it about, by distributing through the pile a small amount of nitrogenous fertilizer such as sulfate of ammonia, together with some ground limestone to reduce acidity and so hasten decomposition.

A simple way to make a compost pile is to spread the raw material on a flat piece of ground to a depth of about 8 to 12 inches. Over this sprinkle ammonium sulfate at 4 to 6 pounds and ground limestone at 1 pound per 100 pounds of plant material. If it is more convenient, the limestone may be replaced by 2 or 3 pounds of unleached wood ashes. Add another layer of plant material and the correct amount of chemicals and continue until the material is used up and a flat-topped pile is formed. Adding a sprinkling of fertile soil to each layer will hasten decomposition, and, if the material is dry, sprinkle water on each layer. In 3 to 6 months, if the pile has been turned once or twice, it should be ready to be incorporated into the garden soil.

PREPARING THE SOIL

Preparing the soil for planting is most important. Dig or plow the soil in the fall if possible; if not, in the spring as soon as the ground is dry enough. If it is available, spread rotted manure or matter from the compost over the surface before plowing or digging at a rate of 50 pounds per 100 square feet if the soil is well supplied with organic matter or humus. On poorer soils, 100 pounds (or more) per 100 square feet may be applied.

Work the garden to a depth of 8 to 10 inches, and cover all manure or compost after thoroughly mixing it with the soil. Turn existing sod under and cover it completely. If quack grass is present use a digging fork to shake out the roots. Thoroughly pulverize and smooth the surface of the soil in order to obtain a uniform stand of plants from seeds or transplants.

GARDEN LAYOUT

If at all possible plan the garden so that the tall plants, such as corn, staked tomatoes, and pole beans will be at the north side where they will not cast shade on smaller plants. It is advisable to run rows across a slope to help prevent water runoff and soil erosion.

To allow for cultivation, place asparagus, rhubarb, and other perennial vegetables on the edge of the garden, about 3 feet from the grass line. Plant the vine crops in the centre, and the other crops on each side with two rows of early vegetables along the edges of the vine crops. These will be out of the way when the vine crops spread later in the summer.

A square or almost square garden is usually easier to handle than a long, narrow one. However, if a garden tractor is used, more headland space will have to be sacrificed. If possible, rotate the different plantings so that crops will not be on the same ground year after year. It is particularly important to rotate such crops as cabbages and turnips to keep clubroot in check. Onions and as a rule vine crops, may, however, be continued on the same soil year after year.

SEEDS AND SEEDING

Good seed is essential for a good garden. The cost of seed, compared with the value of the vegetables harvested, is small, so do not buy cheap seeds. In localities where there is no separate seed store, local stores usually have packet display boxes, but before buying these, make sure they have not been left over from the previous year.

Some seeds are extremely small and consequently very small quantities are needed for the average garden. For example, with cabbage there may be as many as 8,500 seeds, tomatoes 10,000, and celery 60,000 seeds per ounce.

Sow only enough to ensure a good stand of plants. Thick sowing wastes seed and increases the labor of thinning. Stretch the garden line tightly to mark the row and open a drill by driving the corner of a hoe or square stake along the line to the required depth. Make the drill of even depth so that uniform germination of the seed will be obtained.

Place large seeds, such as beans and peas, individually at the specified distances. Sow small seeds, such as carrots and lettuce, by tearing off a corner of the envelope, holding the packet horizontally, and gently tapping it with the finger as it is moved along the drill. Press the soil firmly over the drill after the seed has been sown.

Extend the season of crops by sowing several varieties to mature at different times. Or, sow successive crops after the early crops have been harvested.

When the seedlings are well up, thin the plants to the distances recommended in the table on page 163. Do this on a dull day or in the evening when the soil is moist.

CULTIVATION

Begin hoe cultivation as soon as rows of young seedlings appear, or immediately after the young plants are set out. Kill weeds while they are still small before they can use up plant food and moisture.

Hoeing in bright sunshine will destroy weeds completely, but pull large weeds from the crop rows only when the soil is moist, otherwise the plant roots may be dried out. Avoid working among such plants as cabbage and beans when they are wet, as there is danger of spreading plant diseases.

For good results cultivate the ground once a week to a depth of 1 or 2 inches. As the plants increase in size and cover the earth, hoe less of the space between the rows and decrease the depth of cultivation to avoid injuring the roots. If you cultivate by hand develop paths through the garden and work and handle the plants from these.

GROWING TRANSPLANTS

The seed for transplants is usually started in a hotbed. Where a hotbed is used for starting early plants, place it in a sunny location, preferably on the south side of a building, where it will have some protection. The hotbed can be heated in two different ways — either by electric heating cables or with fresh horse manure.

The Hotbed

Start the hotbed by digging a hole or pit 2 feet deep and filling it with heating manure. Or, if you wish to develop the hotbed on the surface, make the bed of the manure 6 to 8 inches wider than the frame all around, and build it 2 to 2½ feet high, depending on when you start it. The frames are usually made to accommodate 4 sashes, 3 by 6 feet in size, made up of lapped glass, 18 lights of 10-by-12-inch glass to a sash. Construct the hotbed frame of planks 12 inches high at the back

PLANTING GUIDE

VEGETABLE	Distance apart Rows (feet)	Plants in rows (inches)	Depth to cover (inches)	Approximate yield (50-foot row)
BEAN (bush)	2	2 to 3	1½ to 2	30 to 50 qts.
(pole)	2	8 to 12	1¼ to 2	30 to 50 qts.
BEET	1½ to 2	1 to 3	½	250 roots
BROCCOLI	2½	18	transplants	30 to 40 qts.
CABBAGE	2½	18	transplants	30 heads
CAULIFLOWER	2½	18	transplants	30 heads
CHARD, SWISS	2	8 to 12	½	use all season
CHINESE CABBAGE	2	12	½	50 heads
CORN	2½ to 3	12 to 18	1 to 2	45 to 75 ears
CUCUMBER	4	12 to 24	½ to 1	100 to 150
ENDIVE	2	8 to 12	¼	50 to 75
HERBS	2	6	¼	
LETTUCE	1½	6	¼	50 heads
MUSKMELON	4	12 to 14	½	75 to 150
ONION	1½	2 to 3	½	50 to 75 lbs.
PARSNIP	1½ to 2	2 to 4	½	150 to 300
PEAS	1½ to 3	2	1½ to 2	20 to 40 qts.
PUMPKIN	6 to 8	36 to 48	1	30 to 50
RADISH	1	1	¼	30-100 bchs.
RUTABAGA	2	6	¼	100 lbs.
SPINACH	1½	4 to 6	½	1 to 2 bushels
SQUASH	6 to 8	36 to 48	1	100
TOMATO (Staked)	2	18 to 24	transplants	150 to 300
TURNIP	1½ to 2	3 to 4	¼	150 roots
WATERMELON	4 to 6	12 to 24	1	75 to 100

PIT HOTBED

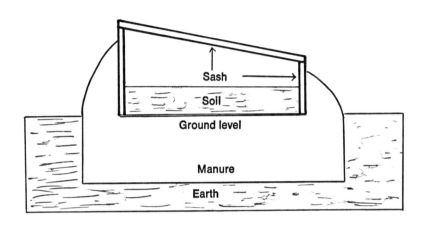

Sash

Soil

Ground level

Manure

Earth

FLAT

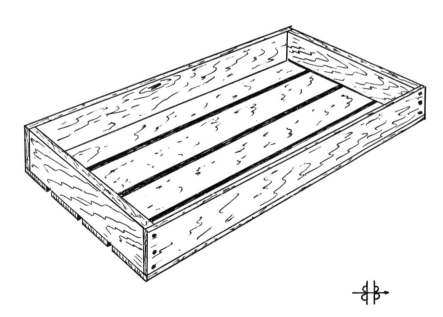

and 8 inches high in the front, in order to give a slope to the glass. Spike in the ends and spike 3 pieces of 2 x 4 inch scantling level with the top of the plank to carry the sashes.

Leave the manure in the pit or pile for 5 to 6 days, then fork it over, shake it out well, and build it up evenly. Water very dry manure to prevent violent heating. Tramp the manure to make sure that there are no slack spots.

Place the sashes and leave them on for a few days; then lift them to allow the gases that will form from the early, violent heating to escape. When the temperature of the manure goes down to about 80°F, place the flats in the hotbed or plant the seed in earth 5 inches deep. If flats are used, less soil is required. Set the flats on narrow boards running across the bed. On frosty nights, with those beds that have little bottom heat, cover the frames with pieces of old carpet, rugs or straw.

Because of the limited air space in a hotbed, the temperature will run up quickly on a bright day, and the plants may easily be ruined by excessive heat. To prevent this, push sashes back for a few inches according to the day and the kind of plants. Tomatoes will stand a higher temperature than cabbages. Water the plants carefully but avoid too high humidity to prevent the development of fungus. Usually the watering is done about noon so that the soil and air may dry out before closing the bed for the night.

The Coldframe

A coldframe is an excellent intermediate stage. Move the plants from the hotbed to the cold frame to harden them for an early planting in the garden. The coldframe is constructed in the same manner as the hotbed but it is placed directly on the soil. If it is ready early, is well banked, and good soil is used, reasonably early plants can be raised.

Close the coldframes early in the evening and cover them with a carpet to prevent loss of heat during the night.

I use flats that are about 12½ x 22 inches, with 3-inch deep sides. The end pieces are made out of ⅝-inch wood and the sides and bottom are made of ¼-inch material. Leave a little space between the bottom pieces to permit drainage. I make all my flats of the same size so that they can be shifted readily or replaced by others. The flats can be used year after year if you store them in a dry place when not in use.

THE HERB GARDEN

Many of the common savory herbs are readily grown on a wide range of soils, but they will generally do best on a sandy loam, and

165

require plenty of sun in order to develop best. A few plants are ample for the home garden. Seed should be sown in the early spring and the plants should later be thinned to about 6 inches apart.

Among the more common and easily grown herbs are the annuals — anise, basil, coriander, cress, dill, and summer savory, and the perennials — chive, sage, and thyme. With the exception of coriander, these may all be used fresh by simply cutting the leaves, and, in some cases, the partly developed flower clusters.

The leaves and fruiting tops of dill are cut when the fruits are fully ripe but still green. Sage should be cut before flowering and may be used dried or fresh. Cress is cut before flowering and may be used dried or fresh. Thyme, summer savory, and basil, if cut for drying, should be taken at the bud or early flowering stage. Anise and coriander are cut for drying when their seeds turn brown. Chives can be used any time in the fresh state.

Plants intended for drying should be gathered before a heavy rain occurs in the fall, because this will cause them to break down and will cover them with sand. They can then be tied in bunches and, for best flavor retention, be dried rapidly in a dry, well-ventilated, dark room. This is particularly true of the more tender-leafed types, which may lose their color if dried in the light.

ASPARAGUS

One-year old plants are usually the best for setting out in an asparagus bed. The plants may be bought from a nursery, or they may be grown in the garden from seeds sown in the early spring in rows 15 inches apart. Soak the seeds for 2 or 3 days in warm water at 80° to 85°F before planting; then sow 2 inches apart in the row and cover with 1 inch of soil. It takes 2 to 3 weeks for the seed to germinate. Thin the plants to 4 inches apart in the row.

Transplant asparagus very early in the spring in rows 4 to 5 feet apart. Choose fresh, vigorous roots and set them 1½ feet apart each way. Place the plants in deep furrows with the crown of the plant 6 inches below the soil level. Spread the roots evenly in all directions and cover with 3 inches of surface soil. Fill the trench in gradually as the plants grow.

No cutting should be done in the first year of growth and only a light cutting, not extending over more than 2 weeks, in the second year. Cutting in succeeding years may be continued for a period of 6 to 7 weeks, to early July. Cutting should then stop entirely to allow the plant to prepare for winter. Harvest asparagus by pushing a sharp knife into the soil directly below the spear, cutting it about 1 inch below the surface. Spears should be about ⅜ inch in diameter, and at least 5½ inches long, with 85 percent of the length of the stalk green.

RHUBARB

Seed may be used and from it good plants can be harvested in the second year after seeding, but such plants often vary in rate of growth, color, and quality. The better varieties may be multiplied by dividing the plant into several parts with an eye and a root in each part.

Prepare the soil thoroughly and deeply; do not be afraid of overfeeding the plant with manure. Plant very early in spring, 4 by 4 feet apart with the eye level with the top of the soil. Do not disturb the plants by deep plowing or working. After the spring preparation, cultivate only enough to control weeds. Grass or lawn clippings can be used to advantage as a mulch around the plants.

No harvesting should be done during the first year of growth and very little, preferably none, during the second year so that good crowns may develop for future crops. Early spring growth depends largely upon the stored-up nourishment in the roots — pulling too many stalks and destroying leaves during the summer and late fall should be avoided. Remove seed stalks before the seed sets.

Drawing and technical information courtesy of Canadian Department of Agriculture, Ottawa

CHAPTER 13

Harvest

After a summer of hard labor the produce that you have so carefully tended must be properly stored and preserved so it will not spoil during the winter months. If your homestead is far from electricity and other modern conveniences, you might have to resort to the early settlers' methods of storing vegetables, fruits, and meat.

STORING VEGETABLES AND FRUITS

First let us classify the different products and where and how they should be stored.

The most perishable products are green peas, green limas, corn, asparagus, and green vegetables such as spinach, chard, and lettuce.

The less perishable are broccoli, cauliflower, late cabbage, and onions. These should be canned in glass jars and kept in a cool but frost-free place.

The keepers are potatoes, turnips, beets, carrots, pumpkins, late squash, celeriac, and the orchard products — apples, pears, cherries, and all wild and cultivated berries.

The Root Cellar

Fruit and vegetables must be properly stored, otherwise they will not keep. By far the best storage room is still the root cellar. No respectable homestead is without one. Have your root cellar ready well before harvest time. Before digging your root cellar know some of the basic requirements for a good one.

The outdoor root cellar should be close to your living quarters. Remember that you will have to get to it even in the coldest weather when there is lots of snow. An earthen floor is best, so make sure that the spot you select has perfect drainage. Just to be on the safe side, install a 4-inch drain pipe all around the foundation. If you have a hill or a slope nearby, this is the ideal place to excavate because a root cellar here is less apt to have any drainage problems. But also remember that during harvest you want to be able to get to the root cellar with the tractor and wagon carrying the products to be stored.

It should have good ventilation that can be adjusted and even shut off at times. It is most important that the root cellar be frost free even in the coolest weather. Double doors placed at least 4 feet apart are necessary to create an air lock, so you can enter through one door and close it before the next door has to be opened. The temperature should be kept as close as possible to 35°F. Humidity of 85% is ideal for most storage.

Make the cellar large enough so that you have room for lots of shelf space, bins for root vegetables, platforms for casks of beef and pork products. (A 12 x 15-foot space is adequate to hold all the storage for a family of four.)

The structure can be made of any one of several different building materials — poured concrete walls, concrete block walls, or, as the early settlers made their walls, of double cedar logs with sawdust filling between the logs. After the walls and a roof of timbers are erected, bank earth on the sides and on the roof to a thickness of at least 3 feet. Cover the whole thing with grass sod or seed it as soon as you are finished with the grading. The sod or the grass will absorb rain and help keep the storage cellar dry.

I have found wooden pallets on the floor to be the most practical floor covering, as they can be removed during the summer and placed outside in the sun to dry.

Bins for potatoes and other root vegetables should be lined with metal bug screening and filled with dry peat moss. I acquire several bales of peat moss early in the summer, take them apart, spread them on a polyethylene sheet, and let them dry in the sun all summer long. When the time comes to store my potatoes I sprinkle enough peat moss between the potatoes so that they do not touch each other. Do the same with carrots, beets, turnips, squash, and celery. Keep apples and pears in wooden barrels filled with dry sawdust. The storage material (the peat moss and sawdust) should be removed from the cellar in the early spring and brought out in the sun to dry. It can be used again the next season.

170

CANNING FRUITS AND VEGETABLES

Two pieces of equipment that will pay for their weight in gold during the harvest season are the tin-can sealer that fits number 2 and 3 cans, and a pressure cooker-canner, equipped with pressure gauge, that will hold 21 quarts.

Organisms that cause food spoilage are always present in the air, water, and soil, as are enzymes that cause changes in flavor, color, and texture in raw fruits and vegetables. To get rid of the unwanted bacteria it is necessary to heat the food to a point where the bacteria are killed. Only then is the food safe to eat after a long period of time in storage. The steam-pressure canner is an easy and safe way to bring the temperature up high enough to destroy the bacteria. A word of warning: keep your steam-pressure canner in top condition. Check the pressure gauge before the canning season, and, if the gauge is out more than 4 pounds, replace it with a new one.

The steam-pressure canner can be substituted for a water-bath canner if used without the lid. Tomatoes and pickled vegetables can be processed safely at lower temperatures due to their high acid content. All other fruits and vegetables should be processed in the steam-pressure canner.

If you are using glass jars, make sure that the lids and containers are in perfect condition, without cracks or chips, and always replace the rubber seals with new ones each time they are used. Sterilize all glass jars before any food is packed in them. If you use tin cans, special R-enamel tin cans should be used for beets, red berries, red or black cherries, plums, pumpkins, rhubarb, and winter squash. Plain tins are suitable for all other fruits and vegetables.

Selecting Fruits and Vegetables for Canning

All fruits and vegetables selected for canning should be as fresh and perfect as possible — firm, young, and tender. They must be canned quickly, before they lose their freshness. Sort for ripeness, and wash well to remove any dirt since it will contain some undesirable bacteria. Never pour the fruit or vegetables from the wash water: lift them out so the washed-off dirt will remain in the water.

The containers can be filled in either of two ways — raw packed or hot packed. Personally I prefer the raw-packed method as this retains all the juices that otherwise would be left in the boiling fluids. Remember when using the raw-packed method, the containers should be packed as tightly as possible because the contents will shrink in the process of boiling.

171

Always make sure there is enough fluid in the cans or jars. A quart glass jar or a number 2 can takes from ½ to 1½ cups of liquid. When raw packed, the fruits or vegetables are packed tightly, then covered with boiling hot syrup or water. Tin cans are sealed before processing, but food packed raw must be heated in the cans (exhausted). To exhaust, place the open, well-packed cans on the racks and fill the pressure canner with water to about 2 inches from the top of the cans. Insert a thermometer in the centre of a can and boil until the reading is 170°F, or for the length of time given in the directions for the fruit or vegetable you are canning. Remove the cans from the water one at a time, add boiling liquid or water to fill to the proper level or head space. Place a clean lid on the filled can. Seal at once.

Processing

Processing is the time and temperature it takes for different fruits and vegetables to be boiled in the pressure-canner after the cans or glass jars have been sealed. When processing take into consideration the altitude above sea level. As water's boiling point is lowered with increased height, you may have to increase processing time accordingly.

Altitude Compensation Chart

Increase in processing time if the time called for is:

	20 minutes or less	more than 20 minutes
1,000 feet	1 minute	2 minutes
2,000	2	4
3,000	3	6
4,000	4	8
5,000	5	10
6,000	6	12
7,000	7	14
8,000	8	16

Processing Times (Raw Packed)

	Preserving	Canning (No. 4)	Canning (No. 2)	
Apples, cored	15 minutes	20 minutes	10 minutes	212°F
Applesauce	10	10	10	212°F
Berries (except strawberries)	10	15	15	212°F
Cherries	20	25	20	212°F
Fruit Juices	5	5	5	212°F
Peaches	25	30	30	212°F
Pears (halved)	25	30	30	212°F
Plums	20	25	15	212°F
Rhubarb	10	10	10	212°F
Sauerkraut	15	20	20	212°F
Tomatoes	35	45	45	212°F
Tomato juice	10	10	15	212°F
Asparagus	25	30	20	212°F
Beans	20	25	25	240°F
Beets, pickled	30	30	30	212°F
Carrots	25	30	25	240°F
Corn, whole-kernel	55	85	60	240°F
Peas, green	40	40	30	240°F
Spinach (and other greens)	70	90	65	240°F

A syrup for fruit will help them retain their shape, color, and flavor. Most directions for canned fruits call for a sweetening in the form of sugar syrup.

A thin syrup can be made from 2 cups of sugar and 4 cups of water or juice. If you prefer a medium-heavy syrup, use 3 cups of sugar and 4 cups of water or juice. A heavy syrup takes 4½ cups of sugar to 4 cups of water or juice. The sugar and water or juice have to be brought to a boil and simmered for 5 minutes.

If you prefer unsweetened fruit, the syrup can be replaced by boiling water. Artificial sweeteners can also be used. Use the amount of sweetener that replaces sugar as directed on the container.

JAM AND JELLY MAKING

Blackberry Jam

1 quart blackberries   **3 cups sugar**

Heat the berries very slowly, then mash them through a sieve. Heat sugar in a moderate oven. Pour the blackberry juice and pulp into a 2-quart stainless steel saucepan; bring to a boil and add the sugar. Stir well and boil very rapidly, watching carefully so it does not burn. Boil until it sets or wrinkles when a little is put on an ice-cold dish.

If you prefer the seeds left in, put the berries into a saucepan; stir and crush with a wooden spoon and boil for thirty minutes, then add the sugar and proceed as above. Pour into small sterilized jars and cover with paraffin or sealing wax.

Currant Jam

1 quart currants   **3 cups sugar**

Wash the currants and pick them free of stems; then measure them, combine with the sugar, and let stand overnight. In the morning bring them to the boiling point, stirring constantly until set. Test as you would for jelly by dropping a little on a saucer and cooling on ice. If it congeals it is ready to pour into sterilized jelly glasses. Place in a sunny corner of your kitchen table. When cool, seal with paraffin or sealing wax.

Rhubarb Jam

3 pounds rhubarb   **¼ pound orange peel**
½ pound figs   **juice and rind of one lemon**
                                  2½ pounds sugar

Cut the rhubarb into 1-inch pieces, chop dried figs into small pieces, grate the orange rind and lemon rind. Add the lemon juice to the rhubarb. Alternate layers of rhubarb, figs, and orange peel; sprinkle a little sugar on top and repeat this operation until all the ingredients are used up. Let stand overnight. Transfer the rhubarb-fig mixture into a 3-quart stainless steel saucepan, place over high heat, and let come to a boil. Lower the heat and simmer until thick, or about 1 hour.

Sterilize jelly glasses and fill with the jam. Seal with paraffin or sealing wax. Store in a cool place.

Strawberry Jam

4 quarts strawberries   **10 cups sugar (approx.)**

Place the berries into a colander and dip it up and down in cold water to wash the berries. Drain and hull the berries. Place 2 quarts of berries in a stainless steel kettle over moderate heat, and mash well. Do not let them come to a boil, but mash and heat until the juices are well started. Measure the pulp and juice. For each pint measured, add one pound of sugar. Add the sugar to the pulp and juice in the kettle and bring quickly to a boil; lower the heat and let simmer for about 15 minutes, skimming the surface until perfectly clear. Add the remaining 2 quarts of whole berries.

Bring to a rapid boil and boil for 5 minutes. If you prefer very thick jam carefully skim out the whole berries and cook the juice for 5 to 15 minutes. Add the berries again and mix well but carefully, so that the whole berries are not broken up.

Sterilize small tumblers and fill with the jam. Place the filled tumblers in a sunny spot; cover with clear glass and let stand for 2 full days before sealing with sealing wax. Store in a cool place. This same basic recipe can also be used for black or red raspberry jam.

Spiced Currants

1 quart currants   **1 tablespoon ground cloves**
3 pounds sugar   **1 tablespoon ground cinnamon**
2 cups vinegar   **1 tablespoon ground allspice**

Wash and stem the currants. Put the vinegar in a large stainless steel kettle and heat over moderate heat; add the sugar and stir until it is dissolved. Add the fruit and spices, bring to a boil and simmer for 2 hours, stirring often to prevent the berries from sticking to the bottom of the kettle. Sterilize glass jars and fill with the berries. Let stand until cool and seal with paraffin or sealing wax.

Ripe berries or gooseberries can also be spiced in this manner and are delicious served with cold meats.

Fruit Jelly

1 quart currant juice   **5 cups sugar**

Select currants, removing any bruised fruit and wash well in cold water. Put the berries in a large stainless steel kettle; leave the stems on but mash well. Place the kettle over moderate heat until the juices are well started. Do not let it come to a boil. Place the fruit in a jelly bag and let stand overnight to drain.

The next morning place jelly glasses in a preserving kettle with a bottom rack. Fill with cold water and let come to a boil.

Measure the juice from the berries — for each pint or quart use an equal amount of sugar. Place the juice in a large stainless steel kettle and bring to a boil over high heat, let boil for 20 minutes, skimming often. After the juice has boiled 10 minutes, measure the sugar into a baking pan and place in a moderate oven, being careful that the sugar does not melt.

After the juice has been boiling for 20 minutes, add the heated sugar and stir until all the sugar has dissolved. If your fruit was not overripe and your measuring carefully done, the jelly should jell on a spoon dipped in cold water. It is now ready to strain into the heated jelly glasses. If not, it must be cooked longer. Set in the sunshine to cool. Cover with melted paraffin or sealing wax. Store in a dark, cool cellar.

Grape, raspberry, and blackberry jellies are made in the same manner. A mixture of fruit juices always makes a pleasant variety. For red raspberry jelly add ⅓ currant juice. For crabapple jelly the addition of wild plum juice or a stick of cinnamon improves the flavor.

PICKLING

Sweet pickles are made from all fruits that can be preserved, such as watermelon rind, crabapples, peaches, pears, cucumbers, and many others.

In all pickling, a good cider vinegar and a careful selection of the very best spices are important. The success of pickling depends mainly upon the purity and flavor of the spices. The syrup for sweet pickles should be rich and thick and cooked well, to keep without being sealed. Do not use preservatives or artificial coloring of any kind if you wish to have a pure-tasting product.

Watermelon, Peach, or Pear Pickles

2 teaspoons ground allspice	4 pounds brown sugar
2 teaspoons cinnamon	2½ cups cider vinegar
1 teaspoon cloves	1 whole ginger root
1 teaspoon mace	7 pounds watermelon rind

Divide the spices into 3 parts and tie each in cheesecloth bags. Put the sugar and the vinegar into a large stainless steel kettle, add the 3 bags of spices and the ginger root broken into pieces. Bring to a boil.

176

Cut the watermelon rinds into 2-inch pieces (lengthwise) and about 1-inch wide. Soak the rind in a weak alum and water solution overnight (one teaspoon of alum per gallon of water). Add the rind to the sugar-vinegar solution and bring to a boil again. Remove from heat, cover, and let stand for 24 hours. Take the melon rind out and let the remaining syrup come to a boil. Add the melon rind again and let stand for another 24 hours. Do this daily for 7 days.

The last time, bring all to a boil, lower the heat and simmer for 15 minutes. Sterilize glass jars, put the rind and syrup into the jars, place lids on top, cool. After they have completely cooled tighten the tops and place in a cool dark place in the root cellar.

Green Tomato Pickles

8 quarts green tomatoes	1 cup mustard powder
3 tablespoons whole allspice	3 tablespoons whole cloves
1 dozen sliced onions	3 tablespoons dry mustard seed
3 tablespoons black pepper	cider vinegar

Wash the tomatoes and carefully remove any dark spots. Slice and place first a layer of tomatoes then one of onion in a stone crock, salt lightly on top of each layer and repeat until all the tomatoes and onions are used. Cover and let stand overnight. In the morning drain off all the liquid and juice. Put the tomatoes into a stainless steel kettle with the rest of the ingredients; cover with vinegar and simmer gently for 20 minutes. Sterilize glass jars and fill with the tomatoes.

Chow Chow

3 cups coarse salt	2 quarts cider vinegar
1 gallon cold water	1 cup brown sugar
1 quart small cucumbers	½ cup olive oil
½ pound prepared mustard	1 head cauliflower
1 tablespoon turmeric	1 quart button onions
2 tablespoons dry mustard	

Heat water just to dissolve the salt; cool. Place the pickling cucumbers in the salted water and let stand overnight. In a small stainless steel saucepan boil the onions; in another pan boil the cauliflower.

Put the cider vinegar into a large stainless steel kettle. Mix the mustard with the turmeric and add a little cold vinegar to moisten the mixture. Add the mixture to the hot cider vinegar and stir constantly until it starts to thicken. Add the rest of the ingredients to the hot vinegar-mustard mixture. Transfer the well-drained vegetables to sterilized glass jars, dividing the cucumbers, onions, and cauliflower as evenly as possible among the jars. Pour the hot liquid over the vegetables and seal while still hot.

Cucumber Sauce

12 large cucumbers	½ cup sugar
salt	1 tablespoon salt
2 quarts onions	1 tablespoon dry mustard
¼ cup mustard seed	4 eggs
12 small red peppers	1 cup cream
1 tablespoon celery seed	3¾ cups vinegar
¾ cup butter	

Chop cucumbers (without paring) and onions finely in a food chopper. Put alternate layers of cucumbers and onions (salting each layer) into a stone crock and press overnight with a heavy weight. In the morning drain the juices off and discard. Scald the cucumbers and onions in enough good cider vinegar to cover. Add the finely chopped red peppers, and mustard and celery seeds, stirring thoroughly.

Cream the butter and sugar, add the salt and dry mustard and stir well. Beat in the eggs one at a time and then add the cream. Add to the vinegar and place in a large stainless steel kettle and bring to a boil. Stir in the cucumber-onion mixture. Mix well and simmer for 5 minutes. Sterilize large glass jars and put the mixture into them. Seal while still hot.

Old-Style Chili Sauce

8 quarts ripe tomatoes	1 teaspoon mace
½ cup strong horseradish	1 tablespoon white pepper
2/3 cup salt	2 small red peppers
2 tablespoons celery seed	1 quart vinegar
1 cup brown sugar	3 large onions
1½ tablespoons ground allspice	

Dip the tomatoes in hot water and peel. Cut them in half, remove most of the seeds and chop fine. Also chop onions and red pepper very fine. In a large stainless steel kettle mix all the ingredients and place over medium heat. Simmer slowly for 3 hours.

Sterilize large glass containers, fill with the chili sauce and seal while hot.

Mixed Vegetable Pickles

8 quarts green tomatoes	1 tablespoon cinnamon
12 medium-sized onions	1 tablespoon allspice
4 green peppers	1 tablespoon mustard seed
salt	1 tablespoon celery seed
2 cups sugar	cider vinegar
1 tablespoon ground cloves	¼ cup salt
1 tablespoon ginger	

Wash and slice the tomatoes, onions, and peppers; place in a large bowl, sprinkle with salt and let stand overnight. Drain off the juices and discard. Place the vegetables in a large stainless steel kettle; add the spices, cover with good cider vinegar and bring to a boil over high heat. Lower the heat and simmer until tender.

Sterilize large glass jars and fill with the mixture, being careful not to break the tomato slices. Seal while hot and let cool in the sun, then store in a cool cellar.

PRESERVING MEAT

Home freezers have changed the preparation and preservation of many of the food products found on the farm. But if you live where electricity is not easily obtained you might have to foresake the conveniences of a home freezer and preserve home-grown products in old fashioned ways. To my way of thinking the old-fashioned ways are not only more economical but the food tastes better too.

There are at least 8 basic methods for preserving meat:

Dry salting
Corning
Smoking
Crock preserving
Pickling
Drying
Natural freezing
Lard packing

All meats — pork, veal, beef, lamb, poultry, and all wild animals can be preserved using any of the basic methods.

179

Curing and Smoking Hams

Hang fresh hams up for a week or 10 days. The longer they hang, the more tender they will be. The length of time they can hang depends on the weather, since they will, of course, spoil more quickly in warm weather. For each ham mix 1 teacup of coarse salt, 1 ounce of saltpetre, and 1 tablespoon molasses. Put the hams in a tub; heat the mixture and rub it well into the hams; repeat this until all of the mixture is used up.

Let them lie in the tub for 2 or 3 days. Prepare a brine of salt and water that is strong enough to float an egg. Pour the brine over the hams and let stand for 3 weeks. Remove from brine and soak in cold water for 8 hours; remove from water and let hang for 8 to 10 days to dry. Smoke (with the hooks down) for 3 to 5 days, being careful not to heat the hams. (Apple or hickory wood gives the hams an excellent taste). Now sew them up in cloth bags and whitewash the bags. Pack the smoked hams in pulverized charcoal in an oak cask, making sure that they are well covered top and bottom with the charcoal powder, and that they do not touch each other.

Old-Fashioned Cured Ham

To each gallon of water add 1½ pounds of salt, ½ pound of brown sugar and ⅛ ounce of saltpetre. Dissolve the saltpetre in a little hot water and mix all the ingredients. Rub the hams with salt. Pack in a well-scalded crock or oak cask, pour the brine over the hams covering them completely. They are ready to eat in 4 or 5 weeks.

Virginia Smoke-Cured Hams

100 pounds of ham	2 pounds brown sugar
8 pounds coarse salt	1¼ ounces potash
2 ounces saltpetre	4 gallons water

Rub the hams with salt, pack in a crock, and let stand for 2 days. Mix the salt, saltpetre, sugar, potash, and water. Pour over the hams and let stand for 6 weeks in the brine. Remove from crock, dry well, and let hang several days before starting the smoking process. The meat should be well cooled before it is rubbed with salt. The potash keeps it from drying up and becoming hard.

Salt Pork for Frying

Cut as many slices of salt pork as needed for breakfast. The night before place the slices in a mixture of half milk and water (skim milk, sour milk, or buttermilk can be used). Rinse the slices in cold water until the water is clear, and then fry. The pork will taste very much like fresh pork.

How to Keep Bacon Sweet (Lard Packing)

After bacon has been cured and smoked, slice it into pieces of serving thickness and fry until a little underdone. Pack the slices in stone crocks in their own fat. To use, slightly refry and serve.

How to Pickle Beef for Long-Term Storage

100 pounds of meat	1 ounce cayenne pepper
fine salt for rubbing meat	1 quart dark molasses
7 pounds coarse salt	8 gallons rainwater
1 ounce saltpetre	

Rub the beef with fine salt and let stand in bulk for at least 2 days to draw off the blood. Mix the salt, saltpetre, cayenne pepper, molasses and water in a large cauldron and bring to a boil. Skim well. Pack the meat in stone crocks, cool the pickling juice, and pour over.

How to Pickle Beef for Winter Use or for Drying

100 pounds of beef	6 gallons cold water
6 pounds coarse salt	

Cut the beef into good-sized pieces; sprinkle a little salt on the bottom of the barrel; pack the beef into the barrel. Mix the cold water and coarse salt and pour over the beef.

The meat can then be used as fresh meat for a long time. When it gets too salty, boil it for stew. If you want to dry the meat, about 3 weeks after you started the pickling, remove the meat to be dried and soak it overnight in cold water to remove the salt. Let dry on drying racks, and it is ready to use.

Corned Beef

100 pounds beef	1 ounce saltpetre
7 pounds salt	4 gallons water
1 pound brown sugar	

Dissolve the saltpetre in a little hot water. Pack the beef as tightly as possible in a freshly scalded crock. Sprinkle a little salt on top. Combine the salt, brown sugar, saltpetre, and water; mix well and pour brine over meat. Make sure that the meat is well weighted down so that every piece of meat is under the surface of the brine.

Dried Beef

Brown salt in the oven on a cookie sheet. Roll the meat in the browned salt, making sure that all the meat is covered with salt. Pack dry in a crock and let stay there for 5 days. Take out, wash well, and hang up on a drying rack to dry.

Bear, Porcupine, and Groundhog meat is treated in the same manner as pork.

Venison, Moose, Elk, and Rabbit are treated in the same way as beef.

CHAPTER 14

Christmas on the Homestead

My childhood Christmases remain vivid in my memory. In our family we celebrated Christmas as it had been for over 300 years. Many of the customs and recipes I describe here date back that far. Here on our homestead many years later we try to recreate the same Christmas spirit.

When I was a boy the preparations for the Christmas celebration started on the eleventh day of November, when the butchering of the meat took place. From that day on, much time on the farm was spent baking and preparing the specialty dishes for the Christmas table.

The Scandinavian custom is to start the celebration on December 13th. On Christmas Eve morning, the family traditionally is awakened early in the morning with coffee and Lucia buns, served by the oldest unmarried daughter in the family, who is clad in white and wears lighted candles in a crown on her head. Traditionally no one eats until the animals have been fed their specially prepared Christmas rations, and sheaves of oats have been placed on long poles outside the windows to give the birds their Christmas meal. At noon the whole family, scrubbed and washed, and dressed in their best clothes, come to the kitchen to taste the Christmas glogg, ham, and sausage.

When we assembled at 4:00 o'clock in the afternoon in our dining-room, we children were enthralled with the decorated table. The Christmas table was set in front of a crackling fire in the open fireplace where the glogg was heated in a freshly polished copper kettle, and the table was laden with the traditional Christmas dishes — the ham and the decorated pig's head, different meat rolls, pickled herring, several different sausages, endless plates of Christmas cookies, and breads made only for the Christmas celebration.

All were softly lighted by gleaming white homemade candles in beautifully carved candleholders. The dim light and the heavenly aroma in the

room set the scene for Santa's arrival later in the evening. (In the Scandinavian countries he arrives in a horse-drawn sled late on Christmas Eve.)

The Christmas table was set on Christmas Eve, and was never removed before New Year's Day. The dishes were taken away at night and replenished to be set out the following morning. Any visitor to the house had to have some of the goodies even if it only consisted of an apple. If not, tradition had it, he would carry away the Christmas spirit.

Glogg (Spiced Wine)

This is the traditional Christmas drink and is served steaming hot. After coming in from snow and cold, it feels like fire going down your throat.

To serve 20 to 25 people

2 quarts dry red wine	20 whole cloves
2 quarts muscatel	1 piece fresh ginger
1 pint sweet vermouth	1 stick cinnamon
2 teaspoons angostura bitters	26 ounces alcohol
2 cups raisins	1½ cups sugar
12 whole cardamoms, bruised in a mortar with a pestle	2 cups whole almonds, blanched and peeled

In a 6 to 8-quart enameled or stainless steel pot, mix together the dry red wine, muscatel, sweet vermouth, bitters, raisins, orange peel, slightly crushed cardamoms, whole cloves, ginger, and cinnamon.

Cover and let stand for at least 24 hours, so that the flavor will develop and mingle. Shortly before serving, stir and bring to a boil over high heat. Immediately remove from heat and stir in the alcohol, sugar, and almonds. Serve hot in heavy coffee mugs.

Lucia Buns

1½ cups milk	1 egg
¼ teaspoon saffron	¾ cup butter
1 envelope yeast	25 almonds
1 cup sugar	5 bitter almonds
2 pounds flour	10 tablespoons raisins

Garnish

1 beaten egg coarse sugar	10 chopped almonds

Dissolve the saffron in ½ cup of warm milk. Mix the yeast with a little sugar and 2 tablespoons of lukewarm milk in a cup. In a large

185

mixing bowl combine the yeast, saffron, milk, and butter. Beat well and add the flour, stirring constantly. Beat the egg and sugar until creamy, work into the dough and allow to rise for 30 minutes.

Scald and finely chop the almonds and work them into the dough with the raisins. Place the dough on a floured baking board and shape into buns. Make cuts on opposite sides of each bun, elongate corners a little, and curl outwards. Place on a buttered baking sheet and allow to rise for 30 minutes. Brush with egg, sprinkle with sugar and chopped almonds, and bake in a hot oven until golden brown.

Christmas Ham

1 lightly salted ham (15-18 pounds)	1 teaspoon whole pepper
8 bay leaves	1 teaspoon allspice
	2 tablespoons salt

Garnish

1 cup dry mustard	¼ cup white wine
1 cup brown sugar	1 cup bread crumbs

Place ham fat side up in a large kettle with a rack on the bottom. Add the bay leaves, pepper, allspice, and salt, and cover with cold water. Bring to a boil, reduce heat, and skim off any foam. Cover and simmer for 3 hours. Turn ham over and simmer for another 3 hours. Pierce the ham with a fork. If clear juice emerges from the punctures, the ham is done. Remove from stock but do not throw away the stock. Let the ham cool, skin, and remove all loose fat. Return ham to stock and let stand overnight. Remove ham from the stock in the morning; set the stock aside and wipe the ham dry.

In a small mixing bowl mix the dry mustard, sugar, and wine. Mix until smooth. Brush this paste all over the ham; sprinkle generously with bread crumbs. Place the ham on a large pan and bake in a low oven for about 1 hour or until the ham is golden brown. Cool. Place on a platter, and in the small end insert a large carving fork with the handle decorated with white and red crêpe paper. Carve thinly and serve cold with hot mustard.

Bread Dip for Christmas Eve Luncheon

the remainder of the juice from the ham (above)
½ cup Christmas glogg

Place the cooking juice from the ham in a large kettle and heat slowly; add the glogg. Cut up 2-inch pieces of potato sausage and pork sausage. Add to the juice and heat thoroughly.

186

Dip thin slices of rye or white bread in the cooking juice. When the bread is well soaked, remove with a slotted spoon and serve on a dinner plate surrounded by a few pieces of sausage and one slice of ham.

Potato Sausage

½ pound ground round steak   2 tablespoons salt
½ pound ground pork shoulder   2 teaspoons white pepper
5 cups ground raw potatoes   sausage casings
  milk

In a large bowl mix the ground steak, pork shoulder, raw potatoes, and the salt and pepper. Add just enough milk to make the mixture soft. Fill the casings partly full and tie the ends.

Place in salt brine strong enough to float an egg. Remove from the brine 1 hour before use, rinse well, and place in a saucepan. Cover with cold water, bring to a boil, lower heat, and simmer for 45 minutes. Prick the casings with a fork to prevent them from breaking.

Spiced Meat Roll

Cut flank steak into pieces 9 inches long and 7 inches wide. On each piece place smaller pieces of veal and pork. Season with salt, pepper, ginger, and ground cloves. Shape into rolls as you would a jelly roll. Sew each roll firmly with cord, so it will keep its shape. Make a solution of ½ pound salt and ¼ cup brown sugar boiled together in 2 quarts of water. When cold, pour over the rolls. Place in a stone crock and leave in the brine for at least 2 weeks. The day before the rolls are to be used remove from the brine and place them in a saucepan with slightly salted boiling water.

Prick with a fork during the cooking. When done, remove from kettle, place between two boards, and put a heavy weight on top. Let stay in press until cold. Slice thinly and serve cold.

Head Cheese

3 pounds pork shoulder   1 teaspoon allspice
3 pounds veal shoulder   1 teaspoon ground cloves
1 tablespoon salt   4 bay leaves
1 teaspoon pepper   1 envelope gelatin

Place the meat in a large kettle and add the salt, pepper, allspice, ground cloves, and bay leaves. Bring to a brisk boil, lower the heat, and simmer until the meat falls away from the bones.

Remove from heat, strain the cooking juices, and set aside. Cut the meat into small pieces and pass through a meat grinder. Put the cooking juices back in a large kettle, bring to a boil, lower the heat, and simmer for 10 minutes. Remove a cupful of fluid and dissolve the gelatin in it. Add the ground meat to the juice and let simmer until well heated. Add the gelatin mixture; stir well. Pour into molds and let stand in a cool place overnight. The head cheese should have jellied by morning. Do not freeze but refrigerate. When ready to use, dip the molds in hot water and turn the head cheese out on a serving platter. Garnish with pickled beets.

Mustard-Basted Spareribs

4 pounds of spareribs	1 teaspoon black peppercorns
1 tablespoon salt	3 bay leaves

Basting Liquid

1 cup dry mustard	¼ cup white wine
½ cup brown sugar	

Crack and cut spareribs across into 4-inch lengths. Bring 2 quarts of water to a boil in a large kettle; add the spareribs, salt, pepper, and bay leaves. Lower the heat to a slow simmer and skim off the foam. Cover and simmer until the spareribs are just done.

Remove from the cooking fluid and drain on paper towels until dry and cool. Mix the dry mustard, sugar, and wine in a small mixing bowl. Coat the spareribs on both sides with the mustard mixture and place on a rack in an oven pan. Broil until golden brown, turning once to get the coating browned on both sides. Cool. Cut the spareribs into individual pieces.

Swedish Meatballs

3 pounds round steak, ground	1 cup minced onion
6 slices white bread, crusts removed	½ teaspoon white pepper
	2 teaspoons salt
3 eggs	4 tablespoons butter
1 cup cream	

Shred the bread and mix with the eggs and cream. Beat with a spoon; soak for 1 hour. Add the salt, pepper, minced onion, and ground meat.

Work well with your hands until the mixture is smooth. Place a large iron frying pan over high heat and melt half the butter in it. Form small, round balls of the mixture with your hands and place in the pan. Shake the pan constantly to prevent sticking. When the meatballs are brown, transfer them to another pan and finish cooking in butter. Serve hot on the Christmas table.

Pickled Herring

Pickling Liquid

1½ cups white vinegar   1 cup sugar
 1 cup water

 1 medium carrot, peeled and   2 small red onions, peeled and
    thinly sliced   thinly sliced
 4 salted herring, 1 to 1½ pounds   2 tablespoons black peppercorns
    each, cleaned, scraped, and   2 tablespoons whole mustard seed
    washed   3 large bay leaves

Bring the vinegar, water, and sugar to a boil in a 2-quart stainless steel saucepan, stirring constantly until the sugar has completely dissolved. Remove from heat and cool to room temperature.

Wash the herring in cold water and cut into 1-inch pieces. Arrange a thin layer of onions in a 2-quart glass jar, top with a few slices of herring and carrots and scatter the pepper, mustard seed, and bay leaves all around. Repeat until all the ingredients have been used, making 3 or 4 layers.

Close the jar securely and refrigerate for at least 48 hours. Serve from the jar.

Christmas Pudding with Almonds

 1 quart milk   ¼ cup sherry
3½ tablespoons sugar   2 teaspoons vanilla
 ¾ cup long-grain white rice   1½ cups heavy cream, chilled
 ¾ cup almonds, blanched and
       chopped

Bring the milk to a boil in a 2-quart saucepan and add the sugar and rice. Stir briefly, then lower the heat and simmer uncovered for about

30 minutes, until the rice is cooked but not sticky. Pour the rice into a shallow mixing bowl and cool quickly. Add the chopped almonds, sherry, and vanilla. Stir well.

In another mixing bowl, whip the cream until it thickens and holds its shape. Fold the cream into the rice mixture, turn the pudding into a mold, and chill before serving. This ancient Christmas dish is served with heavy cream and with a small glass of cherry liqueur poured over. Traditionally a small bowl of this rice is placed outside to please the Gnomes who are believed to live around a good house and to ensure their help for the coming year.

Several kinds of cheese also have a place on the Christmas table, as well as different kinds of herring. At least three varieties of bread are offered — light or dark rye, white bread, and hardtack. Cookies and fresh fruits round out the feast.

Index to Recipes